REPAIRING THE CRACKS WITH GOLD

A STORY OF OVERCOMING EMOTIONAL ABUSE

BARBARA VON METTENHEIM, PHD

von Mettenheim Publishing
Washington, DC

Published by
Hasmark Publishing
www.hasmarkpublishing.com

Permission should be addressed in writing to:
Barbara von Mettenheim, PhD at
Support@Repairingthecrackswithgold.com

Editor: Sigrid Macdonald, Book Magic, http://bookmagic.biz

Book cover: Needava.com

Layout Artist: Anne Karklins, annekarklins@gmail.com

ISBN 13:978-1-989161-23-4
ISBN 10: 1989161235

Printed in the United States of America
First Edition June 2018

www.barbaravonmettenheim.com

This book is dedicated to my lovely daughter, Ashley, who taught me how to love.

Acknowledgments

To Barbara Daoust, my faithful coach, who labors with me as I continue to birth my new life.

I want to thank Bob Proctor who has taught me so much. Bob's energy and relentless enthusiasm for learning inspires me toward my greatness.

I also want to thank Bill Wilson, Dr. Bob Smith, Jim Bunch, Phil Black, Christy Whitman, and Tony Robbins. I couldn't have done it without you all.

I would also like to thank Dr. Jussi Eerikainen. Dr. Eerikainen continues to teach me about energy and its healing properties

Thank you to Margaret "Sam" Sansom who pored over every word fixing my typos and awkward language. Sam shaved her head in solidarity with me when I lost my hair during chemo-therapy. No one has ever done such a loving thing for me. You are the best, Sam.

CONTENTS

Other People Judge Us for What They
Do Not Understand 1

We Are Not Like Other People 4

You Will Continue to Go Back Until…! 11

What Turned the Corner for Me? 13

I'm Outta Here! 28

My Academic Miracle 32

Getting Sober Was Not Enough 43

On My Own at Last! 49

My Trauma Recovery Begins in Earnest 51

Three Years Later 54

How Do We Change the Instructions in the
Subconscious Mind? 56

What You Need Are Super Powers! 57

The Super Power Imagination 58

    Your Imagination Can Communicate with You! 59

    The Cave Vision 60

    How to Direct Your Imagination 62

    Begin Telling a New Story! 62

    Exercise 63

The Super Power Will 65

    Exercise 67

The Super Power Perception 68

    Exercise 68

The Super Power Reason 69

    Exercise 70

The Super Power Intuition 71

The Super Power Memory 73

    Exercise 74

Other Techniques I Used to Help Free Myself! 75

    Find a Champion! 75

    Ask Yourself, "Does this Make Me Feel Powerful
    or Powerless?" 76

    Forgiveness 77

    Figuring Out What You Want! 77

    We Should All Earn Lots of Money! 80

So Where Do You Start? 82

    Take Action! 84

    What Do You Need to Change? 84

    Repetition Is Key 87

    Written Goals 87

    Vision Board 88

    Practice Daily Affirmations 88

    Binaural Frequencies 92

Healing the Post-Traumatic Stress 96

    Identifying Triggers 97

    Other People's Energy Can Trigger a PTS Episode 98

More Techniques to Dispel PTS   100

Praying for People You Resent   100

Recalling Energy from Bullies   101

Analyzing Dreams and Visions   102

Practice Gratitude   103

Stop Comparing Your Insides to
Someone Else's Outside!   103

Avoid Negativity   104

Seek Out Like-minded People   105

Grow Spiritually   105

Practice Compassion   106

Be Kind but Take No Shit – Practice Assertiveness   106

Thoughts That Don't Serve Us   109

Making Shit Up and Believing It!
Stop Catastrophizing   109

"Poor Me"   110

Another Thought Pattern That Does Not Serve Us –
"Bad Me"   112

Another Though Pattern That Doesn't Serve –
Perfectionism   113

Expect Backslides   115

A New Me   117

A New You   121

KINTSUKUROI – GOLDEN REPAIR

"Translated to 'golden joinery', Kintsugi (or Kintsukuroi, which means 'golden repair'), is the centuries-old Japanese art of fixing broken pottery with a special lacquer dusted with powdered gold, silver, or platinum. Beautiful seams of gold glint in the cracks of ceramic ware, giving a unique appearance to the piece.

This repair method celebrates each artifact's unique history by emphasizing its fractures and breaks instead of hiding or disguising them. Kintsugi often makes the repaired piece even more beautiful than the original, revitalizing it with new life."[1]

I have learned to see the beauty in the cracks in my soul. Adversity made me a better, more loving and more compassionate person.

1. https://mymodernmet.com/kintsugi-kintsukuroi/

Other People Judge Us for What They Do Not Understand

Whenever someone hears about an abused woman who goes back to her abuser time after time, the question always arises, "Why doesn't she just leave him?" To people who have never been abused, it seems perfectly obvious that staying or leaving and going back into the situation is the height of insanity. The answer to them is simple – just stop. Yet after a lifetime of having gone back or chosen situations which showed themselves to be just as abusive as the last time, I finally understand why I kept going back.

Fifty years ago, as I was exiting the abusive situation I was trapped in, psychiatry and psychology didn't know how to treat post-traumatic stress. Since the Vietnam war, researchers began studying the soldiers returning from the war with "battle fatigue" as they called it back then. Today there is a body of research that is beginning to scratch the surface of healing post-traumatic stress.

I did not have the benefit of that research. I had to find my way to health on my own, using both accepted and quite non-traditional methods. What I have put in this book is what has worked for me. There was a lot of stuff I tried that didn't work. This book is about what I did to find a safe place inside my own head. This is about what worked for me.

I intend to explain why I continued in these relationships, why I did not even know I was doing it, and why choosing a different kind of person just was not possible. I also intend to provide the roadmap that I followed which led me to make better choices.

I finally left the abusive situations with the commitment never to return. I choose to live alone until such a time that I no longer choose the abuser, the bully, the narcissist, and the person who must belittle me or make me feel small for them to feel good about themselves. I have also let go of both male and female friends who always had to have the upper hand in the relationship. I will never again let anyone, including myself, harm me, push me around, or tell me I do not have the right to be me.

Today I am friends with people who are glad to see me, who think I have something to offer the world, and who treat me with kindness, love, and respect. I have only lately been able to show these behaviors to myself. Once I was able to give them to me, I was able to allow others to give them to me.

Once I understood that I was the common denominator in all these situations and that I kept choosing the same kind of person, only then was I able to begin to put myself first. I have since walked away from almost all the people I had in my life, and I have spent much time alone before I changed enough to be able to surround myself with supportive, caring people who respect and love me.

I used to revile myself for the brokenness that seemed to define me. I titled this book *Repairing the Cracks with Gold* as an homage to the Asian artisans who practice Kintsugi – the art of repairing broken pottery with lacquer mixed with gold. They believe that the breakage and repair is part of the history of an object. Rather than hiding the fractures, they emphasize them believing that the repaired damage brings a new depth of beauty to the object. Today, I view my emotional scars with kindness knowing that I wouldn't have the depth of character and integrity I have today without having gone through the crucible. I certainly would not have the courage to write this book in the hope that I can help someone move even one step closer toward her or his highest good.

WE ARE NOT LIKE OTHER PEOPLE

Non-abused, non-traumatized people do not understand our behavior. They think that they can impose on us their point of view because to them it just makes sense. They cannot imagine what we have gone through, and therefore, they are unable to understand what has happened to us. We are no longer like other people. We are different now. A Abuse and trauma changed the architecture of our brains, and our brains are no longer like the brain of a non-abused person.[2] Once traumatized, the brain, separate from the mind, focuses on the trauma and does not allow the person to experience life the way they once did. The survivor now focuses on living life while trying to contend with the chaos that lives in their brain. The stress of living with the chaos creates a constellation of physical symptoms and a cascade of toxic emotions.[3] We end up with autoimmune diseases, cancer, chronic illnesses, and allergies because of toxic emotions like anger, jealousy, grief, fears and phobias. While others live their lives unafraid and relatively calmly, the traumatized person exhausts the mind and the body trying to present a normal exterior while his/her chaotic interior thwarts all efforts.

What we resist persists. Suppressing the chaos, pretending it is not there, only makes things worse. Even if we are saying with our conscious mind, "I do not want to live in chaos," we

---

2. *The Body Keeps the Score: Brain, Mind, and Body in the Healing of Trauma*, Van der Kolk, Bessel A. - Penguin Books – 2015. P.53 After trauma, the world is experienced with a different nervous system.
3. *The Body Keeps the Score: Brain, Mind, and Body in the Healing of Trauma*, Van der Kolk, Bessel A. - Penguin Books – 2015. P.53 These attempts to maintain control over unbearable physiological reactions can result in a whole range of physical symptoms, including fibromyalgia, chronic fatigue, and other autoimmune diseases.

continue to get that chaos. Our subconscious mind receives input in the form of images from the conscious mind. The mind cannot produce an image of "no chaos." When the conscious mind is thinking no chaos, the image it is sending to the subconscious mind is that of chaos. The job of the subconscious is to give us what we ask for, does not hear "Do not live in chaos;" it only senses "chaos" and serves us up as much chaos as it can. The more it gives us, the more we focus on it, the more it gives us. The vicious cycle spirals around and around until we contemplate the ultimate solution.

Because our subconscious mind is focused on chaos, we find ourselves in circumstances that would appall the normal person. Van der Kolk writes, "Many traumatized people seem to seek out experiences that would repel most of us, and patients often complain about a vague sense of emptiness and boredom when they are not angry, under duress, or involved in some dangerous activity."[4] I never understood why I was drawn to the "bad" kids in school, the slackers, the stoners, the rebels, and the underachievers. I felt the familiar chaos with the kids with those behaviors. I felt that I fit in. I certainly did not feel that I fit in with the regular kids, the ones who had a safe and quiet place to live, the ones whose parents supported them. Their laughter and confidence intimidated me. I needed the feeling of danger.

A girl in my class found herself pregnant. She left home because she was ashamed. My friend told me when her father found her, he hugged her and told her they would get through it. Are you kidding me? If my father had found that out about me, he would have beaten me "within an inch of my life" as he liked to threaten me. Yeah! I didn't fit in with those other kids.

Gabor Maté, a Hungarian-born Canadian physician with a special interest in childhood development and trauma, writes,

4. *The Body Keeps the Score: Brain, Mind, and Body in the Healing of Trauma*, Van der Kolk, Bessel A. - Penguin Books – 2015. P.31

For those habituated to high levels of internal stress since early childhood, it is the absence of stress that creates unease, evoking boredom and a sense of meaninglessness. People may become addicted to their own stress hormones, adrenaline and cortisol, Hans Selye observed. To such persons, stress feels desirable...[5]

This explains why the abused person continues to repeat the behavior of allowing the abuser back into her life. It feels right; it feels exciting; it feels meaningful, even though it is bad for us. I knew a woman who would only go out with guys who had "it." I watched her over the years with the guys who had "it." It turns out that "it" was narcissism. She had no interest in those guys who didn't have "it." I only learned what "it" was after I came to understand what I was doing.

I stayed for years in an extremely stressful marriage and only became willing to leave when my body finally gave out. Toward the end of my marriage, I developed a serious, stress-related, autoimmune illness. After that, I found myself in another relationship with an abusive man. During that long-term, stressful relationship, I developed cancer.

The only thing that has saved me throughout my life is a strong sense of self-preservation and not being afraid to walk away. I want to live. I want to watch my grandchildren grow up. I have things I want to accomplish. I choose not to give in to my addiction to stress, adrenaline, and cortisol any longer. Yes, I miss that delicious feeling; perhaps I am too exhausted or just too old to engage it any longer.

Your brain, through its post-traumatic programming, forces you to focus on the abuse and the behavior that helps you deal with it. Your brain is different than it was before the abuse. The abusers did this to you. Nevertheless, it is your responsibility to fix it now. It is not fair. It is just the reality.

5. Maté, G. (2012). *When the body says no: The cost of hidden stress.* Toronto: Vintage Canada.

Trauma changes the architecture of our brains. We no longer have "normal" reactions to the world; we now see everything that happens to us through the lens of the traumatic experience. If this experience happened early enough and has been long lasting and all pervasive, the brain maybe did not even have a chance to provide us with a snapshot of what we were like before the trauma. We may feel like we are just broken and always have been. The post-traumatic responses in the brain become the default settings.

Research shows that brain synapses produce pathways through the neurons that become paths of least resistance.[6] The brain is always trying to automate processes in order to optimize the use of energy, allowing us to create ways to easily navigate our daily chores. The brain of the traumatized person is trying its best to deal with the world while attempting to manage the fear that governs his/her life. van der Kolk discovered that "Neurons that 'fire together, wire together.'"[7] The synapses actually form pathways, ruts if you will, in our brains. The expression "stuck in a rut" is appropriate to this discussion. The brain synapses are literally stuck in the pathway that the trauma created. This pathway can become the default setting of your thinking.

We have known for a long time that what we focus on gets stronger. The brain has a function called the Reticular Activation System or RAS. The RAS is located in a bundle of nerves in our brain stem that helps filter information so that we only focus on what is important to us. Once we learn something new, the RAS allows it to become part of our consciousness, and we begin to see that it was there in front of us the whole time.

---

6. *The Body Keeps the Score: Brain, Mind, and Body in the Healing of Trauma*, Van der Kolk, Bessel A. - Penguin Books – 2015. P.56 When a [brain] circuit fires repeatedly, it can become a default setting – the response most likely to occur. If you feel safe and loved, your brain becomes specialized in exploration, play, and cooperation; if you are frightened and unwanted, it specializes in managing feelings of fear and abandonment.

7. *The Body Keeps the Score: Brain, Mind, and Body in the Healing of Trauma*, Van der Kolk, Bessel A. - Penguin Books – 2015. P.56

We have all had the experience of learning something new and then seeing evidence of that lesson everywhere. Several years ago, my daughter showed me a new game on my phone. "How do you not know about this game?" I asked her. "Everyone is playing it," She said. Once she showed me the game, I learned that, indeed, everyone was playing it. Over the course of the next few weeks, rarely a day went by that I did not hear someone talking about it. I even heard characters on a TV show talking about it.

When our brains force us to focus on the trauma and our responses to the trauma, our RAS causes us to see the trauma everywhere. We are not defective. Our brains are working just the way they should. That does not mean that they are allowing us any freedom or happiness. We are habituated to the feelings, so we never have the desire or think to get out of our situation. Some of us die in the situation. I finally left only because it nearly killed me.

Traditional therapy fails the traumatized person. Traditional psychotherapy claims that talking about it will eventually release the patient from the situation. However, that is not the case with the trauma victim. The more traumatized people talk about their trauma, the deeper they sink into it and repeat the behaviors. Van der Kolk writes, "Traumatized people have a tendency to superimpose their trauma on everything around them and have trouble deciphering whatever is going on around them."[P17]

Talking about it only makes it worse. Again, van der Kolk indicates, "Scans clearly showed that images of past trauma activate the right hemisphere of the brain and deactivate the left." While we are talking about our trauma, forcing us to relive it, at the same time, we are shutting down the analytical side of our brain that allows us to make sense of what is going on around us. Talking about it keeps us running on the hamster wheel never able to use our higher faculties to lead us toward freedom.

After I was diagnosed with post-traumatic stress and had made significant progress in my recovery, I watched a young woman talk about a stressful situation she experienced in childhood. I was able to observe her in real time as she transformed into that little traumatized girl on the playground. The shape of her face changed, her eyes glazed over, and she withered looking physically smaller as she sank deeper and deeper into the memory. I had seen that happen before though I didn't know what I was looking at. We don't just remember an event. We become the person we were at the time the trauma occurred and we re-experience it anew. At that moment we don't have the analytical side of our brain as an ally to bring us out of it. We are lost in the memory.

∾

I grew up with blame, insults, harsh criticism, humiliation, shame, threats of abandonment, and physical harm. My drunken father choked me with his bare hands. My mother used her children as little human shields against her abusive husband. My father physically brutalized my older sister. As I witnessed the violence and reacted to the emotional abuse I experienced, I withered as a person, as a little girl, growing into a travesty of a human being. I have recovered from the personality traits that caused me to tolerate that behavior from others. It took years – almost sixty years in fact. Nevertheless, I now have self-love and self-respect. Never again will I allow anyone to brutalize me. I hope that this little book can help you arrive at the decision to take care of yourself sooner than I did.

I finally wrote this book after three decades because people kept telling me that I needed to share my story. My excuses for not writing this book were legion. Cue the whiny voice, "But I'm overweight. Who's going to listen to me? I haven't yet found true love… who is going to want to hear that? I'm afraid." These excuses were just my mental paradigms caused by trauma holding me back. Fear still wanted me to hide, to evade the bully, to live in the dark corners of life so as not to be a target of the abusers in this world.

The reality is that I have finally removed myself from relationships where I always lose to the bully. I do not have a perfect life, though I have a highly successful life. I am happy. I am fully self-supporting. I have a good career. I have peace of mind; I have a wonderful daughter who did not suffer through her childhood. I have everything I have ever wanted – I have only ever wanted one thing. I wanted peace of mind!

You Will Continue to
Go Back Until...!

Understand this: You will continue to go back; you will continue to choose the same type of abuser until you finally realize and confront the fact that you must change your thinking. Our abusers programmed our brains to keep us under their thumbs. They brainwashed us to believe that we need them, cannot live without them. They made us believe that the life we lived with them was normal, and if we leave, something terrible will happen to us. We are like the frogs in the pan of water on the stove, which gets hotter by such small degrees that the frog does not notice the heat, and it boils to death. Our subconscious programming draws us to those who are like our childhood abusers.

The abusers taught us to be compliant. Any outspokenness was met with violence. In many books I have read, the underlying story of women, even powerful, highly successful women, is that we are afraid to stand out, afraid people will not like us, and terrified to strike out on our own. Few of us are immune to that fear. Women certainly have a history of being killed for our outspokenness. They burned us as witches; threw acid on us; stoned us to death for violating the rules, for living in our power.

Sometimes they just wore us down until we felt that we did not have the right to exist. Emotional abuse is just as damaging as physical abuse. My boyfriends and husbands never laid a hand on me. They did not have to because I just rolled on my back and showed my belly like a puppy, unable to stand up and fight for myself. I was defeated at such a young age that I never learned I had the right to walk away.

Most women who experienced trauma keep going back or keep choosing partners who have the same abusive characteristics as the last guy or their fathers or mothers. We pity them and wonder why they continue to do it. I was one of them. Now I know why we keep going back.[8] I am no longer doing that. I broke the cycle, and I am free.

You do not have to continue to be one of these statistics. As Eleanor Roosevelt said, "You must do the things you think you cannot do." She also said, "No one can make you feel inferior without your consent." If you are reading this book, you know it is time. You can and must leave and find your true authentic self.

I stayed; I left and came back; time and again, I was further shamed, humiliated, and demeaned. Imagine. It took me five years to get over my affair with a paranoid-schizophrenic-convicted murderer. I thought he was the best. Even now, I miss the last guy, who could be so sweet and wonderful – UNTIL HE WASN'T. Then he would be that sweet guy again, and I would forget about the one whom I called "Satan's asshole."

---

8. *The Body Keeps the Score: Brain, Mind, and Body in the Healing of Trauma*, Van der Kolk, Bessel A. – Penguin Books – 2015. P.53 Being traumatized means continuing to organize your life as if the trauma were still going on – unchanged and immutable – as every new encounter or event is contaminated by the past.

What Turned the Corner for Me?

Pain and sickness. I was sick and tired of hurting and feeling humiliated. I had two serious life-threatening illnesses. What was next – I drop dead of a heart attack? I am not ready for that.

What ultimately helped me were people with a powerful message of ignoring the old story and creating a new one … a story that frees us from past hurt and self-hate. Science proves that you can rewrite your story and break free. Self-loathing is a learned behavior. What the brain learns can be unlearned due to something called neuroplasticity – the ability of the brain to rewire itself, no matter what your age.

Rewiring your brain and breaking free is not easy. It takes time and much work. If you are diligent, eventually you will stop choosing the wrong people, as I did for years, and come out on the other side with your authentic self fully salvaged from the wreckage of the past.

Somewhere in the literature of Alcoholics Anonymous, it says something like this: "All alone and in the light of [our] own circumstances, each of us has to develop the quality of willingness." If you are reading this, chances are you have or are developing that willingness.

You can break free from patterns of thinking that cause you to need an abusive partner. You can reclaim your own self in all its manifestations. To quote a former teacher of mine: "You don't have to believe me, but you do have to believe the evidence."

If my story does not inspire you to seek your true self, keep looking for what will. Freedom is your birthright, and I encourage you to grab hold of it.

～

My story is simple. Born to two narcissistic, spoiled brat alcoholics, I was the second child. My role in this travesty of a family was the scapegoat.[9] I was and am highly sensitive and emotional. My only desire as a kid was to be good. I wanted to be a good girl and a smart girl. The role assigned to me at birth in this dysfunctional family was that of the scapegoat. As the scapegoat, it was my role to take the blame. From my earliest days on earth, it was my fault that everyone's life was so miserable. I accepted that I was the bad girl in the family even though it made no sense. I was too terrified to ever do anything wrong.

It turned out to be a blessing being the scapegoat because, never having been truly accepted into the family, the scapegoat is able to walk away. She may carry scars for the rest of her life, but she has the possibility of escaping.

My father was a dumb, good looking, alcoholic bully. He was a narcissistic snake and possibly the most vicious person I have ever known. He was the only child of an old-world style German milkman and a housewife. My grandmother, after being told she could not have kids, became pregnant and then almost died when my father was born. Unable to have any more kids, she doted on him. My grandfather was the neighborhood drunk until my father, at age fourteen, threatened to leave unless he stopped drinking. From that day forward, my grandfather was a miserable, non-drinking, untreated alcoholic dominated by his son.

My grandmother was the only person who had any control over my father. She was the only one who could bring him out of his violent rages. He took his physical violence out on my older sister, whom I watched him beating for the first time I can remember, when I was about three years old. The rest of us only experienced his rages, his derision, humiliation, and demanding nature. He had us all trapped in an unhappy situation.

Having responsibility for the family foisted on my father before he was emotionally able to handle it put him in a position to rule the adults in the family. He came to believe that he was right, everyone else was wrong, and it was going to be his way or the highway. Alcoholism destroyed him – first my grandfather's alcoholism and then his own.

Relatively uneducated, my father performed factory work, and that made him feel powerless and inadequate. He had no standing in the community, and the only way to flex his muscles was to bully the four women in his life: his wife and three daughters. And bully us he did, hardly ever speaking except to bark orders or growl at everyone. Women were to be at his beck and call and serve him as my grandmother had.

J.K. Rowling, in her book *The Casual Vacancy*, described my father perfectly in the character of Simon Price. He was a man who ruled his family through "physical terror and ritual humiliation."[10] He beat his wife and humiliated and emotionally tortured his sons just for fun.

My father's opinions and decisions were final. He knew that he knew best. He never took into consideration what the rest of us needed. His needs came first, and his word was gospel. If he thought of it, it was a good idea. If we thought of it, it was a bad idea. He kept us away from our friends, forbidding us to go out with them. He kept us all, his children, angry at one another – divide and conquer was his motto. If he kept us fighting, we would not see that he was weak and mean. And it took me into my forties to completely understand his behavior.

10. Rowling, J.K., *The Casual Vacancy*, Little, Brown and Company, 2012.

Gruff and cruel, he terrified me, and I hated being a kid. Humiliation and defeat was all I knew with him. Whatever we were doing, he would scold us. Whatever we said, he would belittle us. He constantly humiliated us. When I was about ten, I was sitting next to him at the dinner table. I had poured too much milk into a bowl of pudding. I knew that if I put the spoon into it and spilled the milk on the table, he would scold me. I bent over and sipped the milk from the bowl so that I could put the spoon into it without spilling it. The second I put my lips to the milk, he pushed my face into the bowl. In a near panic, I bolted up. "You should have better table manners," my father snarled. I knew he did it just because he wanted to do it. He did things like that my whole life. He was a little boy in an adult body with no control over his anger and pettiness.

We learned never to express our own ideas and feelings; I said only that which accorded with what he wanted. I hated myself for it.[11] We could not express our true, authentic self, only that which would please him.

Yet, there were moments when he threw me a few crumbs, and I relished them. When he was watching TV, I could climb up on his lap, and he would laugh and play with me and be fun. Of course, I was always cautious, on guard for when he would turn on me and push me away or scold me, moments I hated: a father is a father, and the child, no matter how rejected, never stops trying to get her father's love. I could make him laugh. My sense of humor would occasionally rear its head, and I could ease the situation by getting a laugh.

I got better at knowing how to handle him. The secret was to sit still and watch him; in that way, I could pick up the

---

11. *The Body Keeps the Score: Brain, Mind, and Body in the Healing of Trauma*, Van der Kolk, Bessel A. – Penguin Books – 2015. P.13 One of the hardest things for traumatized people is to confront their shame about the way they behaved during a traumatic episode, whether it is objectively warranted (as in the commission of atrocities) or not (as in the case of a child who tries to placate her abuser.) … They despise themselves for how terrified, dependent, excited, or enraged they felt. … Most of them suffer from agonizing shame about the actions they took to survive and maintain a connection with the person who abused them.

"He's going to turn on you" signals. Occasionally, he did push me away and scold me. as I became better able to read his body language, that happened less and less. This set me up for constant hypervigilance. Eventually, I just stayed out of the way, hiding in the basement or in my room reading.

I was always glad when my mother made him a drink, as drinking made him happy, and he would play with me for a long time. The alcohol worked… until it didn't. At some point, he lost the ability to "hold his liquor" and became a violent, dangerous man to his children, at least. He didn't have the courage to take on anyone his own size.

My relationship with my mother was not much better. She was a failed debutante. Her mother was from an upper class, old-moneyed family; her father was a nouveau-riche upstart who earned his money in chewing gum and the stock market. He was an inventor and a drunken philanderer. My grandmother divorced him in an age when divorce was a scandal. My mother's shame over the situation was palpable every time she talked about it. She did whatever she could to hide it and herself.

In the 1930s, coming from a broken home carried a horrible stigma, and my mother told her friends that her father was dead. At her sweet 16th party, which is a debutante ball for those not listed in the social register, her "dead" father showed up with a huge bouquet of red roses in hand. The truth was revealed the he was not in fact dead, marking her as both the daughter of a divorcee and a liar.

At seventeen, she went to a "rest home" for a considerable time. The stress of living with her family got to her. Mother's issues were too vast to enumerate. Raised by emotionally unavailable parents, she had no clue who she really was. The social conventions she learned in childhood gave her no solid emotional footing, and she just became a travesty of a woman and a pathological liar.

She was meant to marry a wealthy man; she chose a working-class guy. No longer a "debutante," she was the wife of a factory worker. She had to work by taking in other people's children during the day. Often there were as many as twenty children playing in our backyard and running through the basement of our duplex. Every morning, five days a week, rain or shine, she collected them in her car.

Mother handled the children very well. They played games, sang songs, made paper cut outs, pasted, and painted. Twice a day, they had playtime outside where they rode bikes and swung on the swings. Then she would pop them all in the car and take them home. By the time she got home at night, she was exhausted and had no time or patience for her own kids.

She was as afraid of our father as we were and continually took his side as he humiliated the children. She was a terrified alcoholic and over eater. She used her children to feed her narcissism and to protect her from our father. She never was able to admit that it was he and not us who made her crazy. Having no clue about her true self helped to derange her.

Mother never wanted to have children. She only wanted our father. She reminded us every chance she got. If we irritated her or did something wrong or just acted like kids, she would get annoyed and tell us how she never wanted us and the only reason she had kids was because our father would have left her if she didn't give him kids. She blamed us for the strife in their marriage. "Your father and I never fight over anything except you kids." "If it weren't for you kids, your father and I would never fight." "If you didn't cost so much, we wouldn't have problems." She blamed us for ruining her life. "You damned kids. I never would have had you. Your father wanted kids and would have left me if I didn't give him children." He wanted three kids, and three kids he got. Their fights, his rages, his lashing out, his cruelty she blamed entirely on her children's misbehavior.

Kowtowing to her husband's wishes aside, they fought about money – having come from the upper class, she could not do without nice things. She wanted more than he could make. This only emphasized how out of touch she was. I guess even though she continually informed us that "money doesn't grow on trees," she must have thought my father should have the made it so.

We lived two lives in our family: the one my father saw and the one we lived when he was not there. We constantly hid our actions for fear of his wrath. Mother let us do things with the stipulation that we never told our father. What idiot would ever do that? She just wanted us out of the house. The hiding left me feeling like a liar. I was never comfortable with the situation because I could get caught and be in real trouble. At the same time, I had to do it to have any freedom whatsoever.

While living in that house was an ongoing nightmare, dinner times were the worst. Every night, we had to eat dinner together.

My older sister's behavior, no matter what she was doing, was fodder for derision. She would get him started, and he would work his way around the table belittling each of us in turn. For me, it was my eating habits. He derided me for being the "fat" one, though I was only a bit plump. He derided my older sister for being too skinny. He got upset because the little one refused to eat anything. No matter what we were, it was not good enough, and it was fodder for his rage. Typically, dinner ended with him shouting at us to shut up. I would begin to cry. "Stop crying, or I will give you something to really cry about," he would bellow.

No matter what we were like, what we did or did not do, he made us wrong. All actions and thoughts were a sin. Once you "sinned," there was no redemption. That was it. He cast us into "outer darkness" never to return. My parents had no concept of forgiveness. They defined us by our misdeeds for the rest of our lives. I saw my sister for the first time in twenty years when I had my own family and was in my forties. She still spoke about my failings and defined me as she had when I was ten. She still treated me as she did when we were little.

Only in the summertime, when mother had no "paying" kids, was she a little more fun to be with, and the screaming would stop, especially when he wasn't around, and she could relax. In the summer, we lived in a house at the shore, swimming, and playing in our little rowboat. We kids would take off and be gone all day. She never had any idea where we were, and she was OK with that. Once we had the motor on the boat, we could go all the way across the bay. Sandwiches wrapped in waxed paper and sodas kept us fed. We never noticed we were hungry until we piled into the kitchen at the end of the day. Then we would whiz through the food like a swarm of locusts.

My father worked in the city during the week leaving us with a much-needed break from him. On the weekends, he would come down to the "shore," as we called it, and we would all spend much time on the boat, which he loved. As long as we were out on the boat, and he had a few drinks to improve his mood, he was tolerable. We were always glad to see the booze come out. Until we weren't.

My older sister was like my father – narcissistic, easily enraged, and blaming everybody for her problems. They labeled her the "smart" one, and she felt she deserved reverence. She was exactly like my father, and she wielded her power over me relentlessly. Her rages also impacted the entire family. The least little infraction of her rules sent her into a rage, and she would scream and shout. If my father wasn't screaming at us, she would be; my younger sister and I walked on eggshells. She screamed because we were stupid. She screamed because no one understood her. She screamed because she could not get exactly what she wanted whenever she wanted it. She was miserable, and I was the cause of her misery, or so she thought. If I didn't exist, she often told me, her life would be great.

My sister's attitude set off my father, and that precipitated the beatings. She would sass him. He would beat her. My earliest memory was witnessing such a beating when I was around three, and she was around six. Mother would do nothing to interfere with his rages. I remember my grandmother often running into our house screaming for my father to stop.

The fear I experienced watching my father's violence created a black hole inside me. The emptiness just got deeper and deeper. I can still have that hole. I am just much better at not diving into it when circumstances set off my triggers.

I thought that if my sister would just learn to shut up, she could avoid the violence. She never let up with her attitude, leaving me in constant terror of the next beating. Their fights were legendary. His rage drove my sister to be more and more combative. She would flare up at the drop of hat. If she did not get her way, she would have a shouting fit. The beatings finally stopped when she was old enough to threaten calling the police, and she had the bruises to prove it.

You might think that my sister and I would have allied with each other against our evil father and rejecting, neglectful mother. Instead, we became arch enemies.

From my birth, my sister was taught to hate me. The family story, oft repeated, told how she dropped me on my head the first time I was put into her arms at three years old. This is not unusual behavior for a three-year-old child. To them this demonstrated how much she hated me from day one. They repeated the story of her saying I ruined her life. It was repeated so much, it became true. It was a shibboleth that defined the relationship between my sister and me.

She tormented me. She would pinch and push me, revile me openly, call me names, and use me. For example, with the promise of something nice, she would lure me into her room, get me to do something for her, and promptly kick me out as soon as I finished, never giving me the promised gift. Desperate to be included, I fell for it every time. I felt left out or, at best, merely tolerated. That feeling followed me my entire life.

We never learned to care about each other and have now been estranged for over forty years. I refuse to let her back into my life.

Since the entire family blamed me for everything, I tried to figure out how to make things better. I tried a myriad of different behaviors seeking to make everyone happy. I ignored my own needs. I became compliant, obedient, and forgiving to stop them from becoming angry and losing control. After all, I thought, if I were a better, smarter, prettier, funnier kid, things would get better. When it did not work, I began to hide and keep quiet. People pleasing became a lifelong behavior for me in all my relationships.

My mother used to brag about how I was such a good baby. I never cried or made a fuss in the playpen. From infancy, I learned that it was futile to cry to get my needs met because my parents would, at best, ignore me or and, at worst, scold and humiliate me.

I read once of an orphanage in Africa that had one hundred infants in small cribs in a large room. The room was quiet – not one baby was crying. When asked why the babies were so quiet, the director replied, "They learned that there is no point in crying; no one is going to come to help them." That story hit me hard both for the sadness it relates and because it struck so close to home. Like those poor orphans, I, too, knew no one was coming to help me.

Early on, I felt helpless. Before I could think, I learned to be passive. Before I could talk, I learned the futility of fighting back to try and better my situation. Before I could reason, I knew intuitively that to survive I had to be a very quiet, good little girl. Such was the way my parents unwittingly used neglect and violence to train me to be that way. I lived in fear of violence and abandonment.

My mother reinforced the good little girl persona in a couple of ways. She knew just how to manipulate me. On one hand, she would use the carrot. She used to tell me how good I was because I never cried or made a fuss. I liked the attention I got from her, so I kept doing that. Then she would use the stick. She told me outright I had to comply completely to their wishes, and especially those of my father – "You never say 'no' to your father," or there were terrible consequences to be paid.

Never one to stand up to him, and protect and support her children, mother would use us as human shields to protect her from my father's anger. I learned to be compliant, to mollify him, to cajole him into being nice to me while at the same time behaving to try to get my mother to calm down. I also learned early on not to rile my sister, who hated me just for being.

I felt that I had to comply or face abandonment by my parents who threatened it continually. Do what we say or "We will put you out of the house!" If you do not behave "You will have to live in the streets!" If you do not do what we tell you, "I'll send you to the home," the family euphemism for the orphanage where my grandmother lived as a child.

Their constant ridicule and derision drove my sense of shame, the sense that I was innately bad. I know now that my parents demanded behaviors from us that we were not emotionally able to fulfill, and they had expectations that were impossible to fulfill, out of which grew my sense of failure. I did not think that I had failed; I knew I was a failure. Now I know that failure was the only response to this scenario.

As the scapegoat does, I lost all psychological boundaries. Their bad behavior was my bad behavior. I owned the guilt for behavior and bad actions that I did not myself take. Acting out toward my sisters in response to their acting out only drove me deeper into a sense of shame and guilt.

This shame led to feeling defective, broken, unlovable, unworthy, stupid, ugly, worthless. I did not think I was making a mistake; I thought I was the mistake. When you grow up, as I did, unable to find the deeply hidden, authentic self, you just live into the false persona your family has assigned you. My authentic self was buried under all the eventual acting out – promiscuity, alcoholism – and I, and the rest of the world, never saw the real me.

I lived with massive insecurity, lack of confidence, and abject terror. These feelings defined me.

We moved from New Jersey to Florida after my first year in high school. The thin fabric of our family life shredded after that. My father was away for the first six months. When he finally joined us, we were used to living without him. He worked late nights, and we rarely saw either him or my mother. We took that opportunity to exert our autonomy. However, I was like the abused dog raised in a crate who, once the door opened, chose to stay inside.

My high school years in Florida were checkered. I seldom saw my parents, so I had lots of freedom. That was super good. And I was in Florida… at the beach!!! I thought I was in heaven.

I began drinking at 16 only to descend quite quickly into alcoholism. I was drinking daily within a few short months. I began smoking at 12. I smoked and drank my way through high school.

I could have cared less about school. I was a mediocre student at best. I spent my time with the slacker kids. We hung out. We skipped school. At the beginning of the school year, we had to get a note signed so that the school would know our parents' handwriting. I signed that note for my sister and me. The school thought that my handwriting was my mother's. My poor sister. When I graduated, she got my mother to sign the note, and she got in trouble with the school for forging our mother's signature. That still cracks me up. Sorry, kid.

A friend's much older brother had a friend to whom I was immediately attracted. He was six years older than me and in college. This was attractive to me on several levels. Now I know that what attracted me was that he had many of the same characteristics of my family. He was ambivalent toward me, which in my delusion meant he loved me. He was controlling, which is the only behavior I knew. And he drank the way I did.

He was three hours away during the school year. He wasn't too close to me. Now I know that I had serious issues with intimacy and could not bear to have someone too close to me, someone that I had to live with every day. Having a long-distance relationship was ideal; and I didn't have to worry about the boys in high school not liking me as they didn't seem to do. I was just terrified of all of them.

Our relationship was one of struggle. He made rules that I fought against. I complied in his presence and did what

I wanted when he was gone. He didn't want me to wear a bikini on the beach. He didn't want me to read books. He didn't want me to go to college. He wanted a traditional stay-at-home wife, which is exactly what my father raised me to be. I went along with this because I thought I had to.

My mother told me I would never get out of her house without getting married. Not understanding that I could defy her and just leave, I bullied my boyfriend into marrying me. He thought he had to marry me because we had done "it."

The October after I graduated from high school, we got married. I was becoming more and more unglued. I longed to be gone. I wanted nothing more than to take off and go anywhere. It did not matter where. I just wanted to get away. Our marriage was a sham. We just drank and smoked. We had no friends in common. We only spent time with his friends. He didn't like my friends or want me to spend time with them. It was a constant struggle. Thank God I never got pregnant. That would have sealed my fate.

One night my husband and I were drinking with my mother and father; we were all well into our cups. It was late, and my father was cross-eyed drunk and staggering. He was railing on and on about something.

Not quite as drunk as my father, I lost my usual good judgment to keep my mouth shut, and uncharacteristically, I said what I really thought about the topic.

My father looked at me, gob smacked that I had the audacity to contradict him. Enraged, he came at me with murder in his eyes. I had never seen such rage before, even with my sister, and I felt more frightened than I had ever been of him in my life. He backed me against the wall and put his hands on my throat, squeezing.

Spewing venomous threats and forbidding me ever to speak again, he grasped my throat tighter and tighter. I looked into his unseeing eyes and felt my breath stopping. This was it. He was doing it; after a short lifetime of guarding my words, I was going to die. I started losing control of my bladder. An electric shock shot through me, yet I somehow had enough breath to croak, "I love you." Instantly, his hand released from my throat. No one had ever spoken those words in our house. They shocked him so much that he let go. Years later I realized they probably jolted him out of the blackout. He turned and walked away. Afterwards, the verse from Proverbs came to me, "A kind word turneth away wrath." It saved my life that night. We never spoke about it.

My mother and husband, sitting on the sofa, did nothing to stop him. I knew that if I did not get away, one of them was going to kill me one day.

If I felt alone when I was growing up, it was nothing compared to the despair and loneliness that settled on me after this incident. I couldn't drink enough alcohol to fill the black hole.

Distancing myself from the family and my husband, I began more and more to spend time with my best friend at her mother's house and later her apartment, the two of us hanging out with the pot dealers and other nefarious characters we met on the beach.

When my mother found out where I was, she came there one day and beat me right in front of my friend and her mother. She told me later that there were chunks of my hair all over the room. She thought it stopped me. Yeah, Mother, whatever!

I'm Outta Here!

Eventually, I left it all behind. I divorced my husband. My friend got her father to handle my divorce. He did it all. I don't remember much about it. I left my family. I left Florida. I took off and went north to New York City. I arrived there the weekend of the concert for Bangladesh. There were a bunch of hippies traveling in those days, and rather than taking up with some seriously undesirable people, I just joined a group of educated, and some not-so-educated, misfits, and I landed in a small city in New England. That wasn't by plan. It just happened. I was like *Cool Hand Luke*. "I never made a plan in my life."[12]

Unfortunately, I had no idea how to take care of myself. I didn't know how to dress, so all I wore were blue jeans and tee shirts. I didn't know how to make enough money. And I didn't know how to protect myself. However, I had three things going for me: I knew how to wait tables, I knew how to type, and I was cute. I had the look. I was tiny with long straight hair. No one ever kicked me out of bed.

People wanted to take care of me. The strangers I encountered were never as mean to me as my family was. Yes, I chose unwisely. Most of my issues stemmed from having no idea how to advocate for myself or voice my wants and needs. That would imply that I knew what I wanted and needed, which I didn't.

My drinking escalated, and within a few years, I was drinking hard every day. During this time, I lived in a shack in the woods with no indoor plumbing, in two different closets

12. Rosenberg, S. (Director). (n.d.). *Cool Hand Luke*[Video file].

in the homes of two different sets of friends, two different warehouses with cold running water and a restroom down the hall, a small mobile home in the woods with electricity and no running water. I schlepped water a lot back then.

The members of the local badass motorcycle club protected me and treated me with kindness. I was like their house cat. They never allowed me to come over when they were on a mad tear. I could visit the clubhouse on regular days and nights. I would help their "old ladies" cook. I was too helpless and innocent for any bad guys to do me wrong. I was like the village idiot protected by the king. They liked it when I would come around because I would cook for them. They also appreciated that I was too delicate to take the full brunt of their behavior and didn't take advantage. As for me, I felt a little safer knowing no one would ever try to hurt me because, although I wore no club colors, everyone in town knew I lived under their aegis. No one dared mess with me.

I had one pair of jeans, only a couple of shirts. People gave me used clothes and shoes. I had no idea how to buy anything. I always had a little money because I waited tables and could do typing jobs occasionally. I never wanted to dress up anyway because it drew too much attention to me.

I spent a lot of time in a drop-in center run by a local church. They did not serve alcohol, and people sat around playing chess and bridge. They would hold Bible studies in the basement. It was a relatively benign place. People drank coffee and played games. There were hardcore bridge players that got a little overheated occasionally. Some of the people there allowed me to hang around with them.

I could be seen wandering up and down the main street never looking people in the eyes, avoiding all people, living like a mouse hiding under the detritus of life. My friend Chrissy took care of me. I appreciated here so much. It couldn't have been easy spending time with an afraid depressed person.

The church finally closed the drop-in center, and many of us hippie types moved to a small bar frequented by a more nefarious crowd of drug dealers, pimps, and whores. I kept my distance from most of them. Having felt like a caged animal growing up, I've always had a fear of being trapped, and the thought of going to jail and being locked in a cell with people you don't know or like was my idea of hell. I was careful never to do anything illegal.

I also drank for a brief period in some of the fishermen bars down on the wharf. Drinking with fishermen is dangerous because they don't ever stop. The boat pulls up at the wharf; they hit the bar and stay drunk for a week until they hit the boat. They sober up on the way out to the fishing spot and fish for a week. They come back and do it all over again.

Drinking with fishermen is worse than drinking with pimps and whores because they have to go to work. Drinking with the fishermen was a very bad thing for me to do because I didn't have the forced sobering up period. Once one group left, another was right behind them, and I began drinking fiercely. I vaguely remember one rainy Sunday afternoon drinking an entire bottle of bourbon by myself. I watched as the bartender poured drink after drink for me out of that bottle. I drank every drop. I was talking to a guy who was telling me about his motorcycle. He asked me if I wanted a ride. "Sure, why not? I'd love to." We were both dead drunk, and we rode that motorcycle on the slick, wet cobblestones in the rain, going as fast as he could. We were lucky we didn't get killed.

I'd been drinking one night with a small group of people and there was one guy who was a pimp. I'd known him for a while and always managed to keep my distance from him. This night he was trying to get me to come his place for a little more partying. My resolve was weakening and I finally said I would go. We walked out into the street not seeing the light had changed. I was in the middle of the lane. I looked up to see this car speeding toward me. I was standing between its headlights. Next thing I know, I'm being pulled off my feet by a guy right behind me. As I turned back to look I saw Fred, the pimp, flying up in the air having been struck by the car. He landed hard on the street. The car that hit him sped off as other cars screeched and stopped.

Poor Fred! The ambulance came and took him to the hospital. He was never the same. I heard that his mother came and took him back to Tennessee or Atlanta. I think I dodged a bullet that night because who knows what kind of trouble I could have gotten into hanging out with Fred.

Social services were available, and I would occasionally talk with counselors. Though they didn't know what to do with me, all my counselors loved to have me as a client since I would tell them openly and willingly everything that happened as I understood it at the time. While they found me entertaining and smart, they could never help me.

One therapist, a married Episcopal priest, fell in lust with me. Here I was trying to get help, and he was telling me how much he wanted to fuck me. Great! Of course, I felt like I'd done something wrong. Back then everything was my fault. This sleazy man, under the guise of a gentle and kind priest, only made me feel worse about myself. And on top of it, I knew his wife.

My Academic Miracle

Around 1975, I was living in a guy's attic. I can't even remember his name. I was alone, passed out on the pallet I'd made for myself on the floor, and I heard a voice calling my name, "Barbara!" I shot up out of a dead sleep and looked around. "Barbara!" No one was there. Now awake, I heard, "Barbara! Go to school!" Clear as a bell, there was someone speaking to me. No one was there. I didn't know about alcohol-induced auditory hallucinations – a symptom of advanced alcoholism.

I sat there, confused. I knew I had heard it. I felt as though God had spoken to me, and I knew I'd better follow his dictates, if I knew what was good for me. Soon after that I felt as though I had a mission. I dutifully walked to the campus of the local university and asked for an application.

I had tried to go to school before. I'd taken a few classes at the community college in Florida. And I'd tried other times after that. I was too muddled to complete the application. This time divine inspiration struck in the form of an idea: "Read the instructions!!" OMG, what a concept! Actually reading the directions.

I laboriously read those instructions, and line by line, I entered the information required. My spirits plummeted when I read that I had to fill in the financial data. Numbers have always baffled me. Although I learned to read eight languages, ancient, medieval, and modern, I cannot balance my checkbook. Out of sheer desperation, I made up the numbers. I just guessed at all of them. Then the instructions said, attach a W-2 form. By some stroke of luck or maybe grace, I had it and I knew where it was.

When I compared the number on the W-2 form to what I had made up, I was only one dollar off from the numbers I made up. The gates of heaven opened. The Seraphim appeared singing God's praises. I KNEW I'd heard the voice of God that night. I couldn't have possibly known what those numbers were. I felt like Isaiah receiving the revelation of Jehovah – instead of words, I received numbers dictated by God – placed on the financial aid form. Wow, heavy stuff at the time.

A student loan from the government set me on my educational path. One day, many, many years later, as I was sitting at my desk at work, now a federal contractor and cyber security professional, I realized that I was working for the organization that had given me my first student loans. I was working at Federal Student Aid, back in the day called Student Financial Assistance. I was overcome when I realized that I was supporting the institution that had very likely saved my life.

In school, I studied Greek and Latin, English, and writing. I enrolled in Greek because it was the only language that hadn't closed when I registered. I didn't know what to expect. The teacher sold us our textbooks for that class. When I opened the textbook that first day of class, I fell in love with the beautiful letters I saw on the page. My Greek professor was a brilliant woman who graduated from Radcliffe and Oxford. I was immediately taken with her.

I loved my teachers. I loved the classes; I never missed a class, and I always took the professors whom the other students thought were too hard. I found them challenging. I didn't mind working hard.

I got the best education I could at a state school. I still drank every day, but the need to study and be clear for class and my love for school mitigated the overwhelming desire for alcohol.

I was a complete contradiction. Hanging out with pimps and whores and having no idea that I was smart. Still essentially living "on the street," I was now reading ancient Greek, Spenser, and Chaucer.

I was determined to make it. I realized that if everything was my fault, as my family led me to believe, I had some control over it. I could quit being a bad person. If I was as stupid as my family said I was, I could learn and get smarter, unlike my older sister, who blamed everyone, especially me, for her woes and therefore never changed.

Living in an abandoned mobile home on a friend's property out in the middle of nowhere in the woods, I went to the city one day. I had to stop at this hooker's house looking for a friend. It was a hot, summer day, and in the sweltering, unshaded concrete driveway, I saw a dog chained up with an empty water bowl. She was hot and panting. A Husky/Samoyed mix, she was very furry. I filled up her water dish and went inside. I found out from the hooker that someone had abandoned the poor dog a couple of days earlier. When I left, I unchained her and took her with me. I just stole her.

I took her from that hot concrete driveway to the cool green woods. She got out of the car, looked around and then looked at me. She had an expression on her face that looked like she thought I was God and had just saved her. I have never seen a creature show such gratitude. She protected me fiercely from then on. No one could get near me until she determined they were OK.

From that moment on, Keesha was absolutely devoted to me. Over the years that she was with me I came to understand that she, too, had been abused. The signs began to pile up. The man who abused her wore cowboy boots and a hat.

He had bushy brown hair. He kicked and hit her. I would watch her react to certain men, and finally put the pieces together. It was pitiful to watch her. I knew why we were together.

I had her for about four or five years. She disappeared two months after I got sober. I'm sure she died. I think she was very sick. The vet didn't have the heart to tell me. It took a long time for me to get over her loss. She kept me alive those last three years of my drinking. She was the only connection I had to life at that time.

During this time, I met "Sam," also known as the "old man." That was what people called him – the 'old man.' "Is the old man coming tonight?" "Where's the old man tonight?" The 'old man' took a shine to me. He was at least in his 60s.

Sam was nice to me and wanted to take me to bed. Has far too old, and I just didn't have it for him. It was frustrating for him. However, he watched over me nonetheless.

He was a criminal. He was not just any criminal. He had the reputation of being one of the best safecrackers in the state; a fact of which he was quite proud. Eventually I came to learn that he had done buckets of time in the state prison for robbery.

Yet he and all the other dregs of the earth in that bar were fine with me. They treated me much better than my family ever did, and I let him take me under his wing. I was cute with sad eyes – a puppy amid a pack of wolves. I was quiet until I began drinking, whereupon I could become very silly and loud-mouthed. Sam used to say that I walked through the world with a shining bubble around me.

Sam had mentioned a guy, whom I vaguely remembered meeting when he was at my apartment one night, and how he would like to meet me. "No, thanks. I'm good. I don't want to get involved with anyone." So that was that. No intro-duction; no complication; bullet dodged. Or so I thought.

One day in June, someone knocked on my door. I opened it, and standing before me was this drop dead gorgeous, tennis jock/altar boy, GQ quality man. "Hi, I'm Jack. The 'old man' introduced us last winter."

He invited me to go to the beach with him. Sure, who doesn't want to go to the beach? So we headed out to the beach in his hot little white Renault sports car, and I was just looking at him, hardly able to breathe he was so good looking.

We had an incredible day. Perfect day. I fell drop dead in love with him. I thought I had found the man of my dreams. He had a steady job, he took me out, and he made love to me like there was no tomorrow. He had perfected it to an art form. And we were blissfully happy… for a while.

As you can guess, Jack was too good to be true. The demons burst on the scene. After long hours of lovemaking, he'd jump up and say, "Well, I can't waste any more time. I've got to get some action."

Waste time! It broke my heart. I was completely in love, and he thought it was wasting time.

He'd be off for days at a time, and soon it became clear that he had other women. I walked in on him in bed with one of them. After I caught him with someone else, he checked my pockets for weapons every time I entered the house.

And this doesn't even begin to address most of the issues. Oh, did I mention that he was a paranoid schizophrenic? He even had another name and apparently a whole other personality that I had never met. Other people talked about him using another name. I only knew him as Jack.

I often wondered if he had multiple personalities. One time he told me that he would often fall asleep when driving. "What are you talking about? How do you do that?" I asked. "I just let the other part of my mind take over, and it does the driving," he replied. Whoa… wait a minute… what other part might that be? I don't have another part that does that. Even I, with my addled brain, thought that wasn't quite right.

Then these guys started showing up at his house. At first, I disregarded it. So, he dealt quarter pounds. Everybody did back then. I found out that he was dealing guns.

I was desperately in love, obsessed in fact. I couldn't get enough of him and our delicious lovemaking; it was torment for me when we were apart. If sex was the only way I could feel connected to another and not so utterly alone, so be it. It's not that I wasn't conflicted because, after all, he was a criminal. I glossed over the fact that he was on parole for first-degree murder. I even wanted to marry him.

He was perfect. He was emotionally unavailable. He seldom talked about anything personal. He was unfaithful to me. He talked down to me. He never wanted to know any of my friends. Why wouldn't a person like me be attracted to him? He was the perfect interplay of abuse and caring that kept me hooked.

One night, we went out to dinner at a beautiful, elegant French restaurant where I used to work, and when we got home, he tried to ask me to marry him, which was all I wanted him to do. Instead of quietly listening to the words I wanted to hear, out of my mouth came a horribly snarky remark, and it was suddenly over.

I now realize that God was talking through me because if I'd married him, it would've been a nightmare, maybe even been the end of me.

I soon learned that he and his buddy were pulling armed robberies right in the middle of town. He would be gone the night before, and then on the news there would be a report of two guys on motorcycles that had robbed this place and, on another night, that place. It was a two-man crime spree all over town.

I knew I had to leave him. Low self-esteem be damned; my conscience got the better of me. I left and went back to Florida for the first time in many years. A few months later, I returned to New England, and he was living with another woman. Still I didn't let go. He continued to come over occasionally, and we would make love, though it was torment for me.

If he hadn't been with another woman and been locked up after he was shot during a robbery and caught, I may never have left him. That's how hooked I was on him.

It wasn't long after that I was standing in the bar one night, and I realized that I was living another night like the previous night, and that every night was going to be the same. Night after night, day after day was going to be the same as every other. And I felt trapped. All at once, I exclaimed, "In three months, I'm not going to be here anymore." I had no idea where that came from or how I was going to change. All I knew at that moment was that I didn't want that life anymore.

I thought about killing myself as there was no hope for me. As that thought took hold, another one came in its place. "If you are going to die anyway, why not die to Christ?" I wasn't sure what that meant or where it came from. I thought, Well, what have I got to lose? There's nothing here worth living for.

And then angels started to emerge.

The first angel was Polly, one of the women from the drop-in center I met when I first got to New England. She prayed for me every day. I would talk to her because she was nice to me. She was a lot like my grandmother, so I loved her. I finally confessed to her that I wanted to die.

She offered to let me live in her home for two weeks on the condition that I went to church every night and severed contact with the street people I knew before. I was too desperate to say "No." I had nowhere to go. And I feared I was going crazy. Everything looked to me like it was molded out of plastic. The trees were molded out of plastic; houses were molded out of plastic. And I had this vision of a wolf-like creature every time I closed my eyes. I was starting to lose touch with reality.

I went to church. I would have done anything she said. I was at the service one evening, on my knees for the prayer. I had never really engaged my own idea of God. I'd been given an idea of God that was distant and apart from me. It was just what you said, that you believed in God. No one really meant it. All at once, a real and earnest prayer occurred to me, a plea to some greater unknown. "God, please draw me to you." I could feel a crack in the shell that was around me. I kept repeating it. The next day I got up, and I didn't cuss – not the whole day – as I had done for years. I didn't try not to cuss. There was just nothing there. I mean nothing… not even "darn." And what was even weirder, I didn't cuss for months and months. Clearly, *something* had happened.

Going to Church

At church, I met another angel. This guy was kind of a lay evangelical preacher. He introduced me to a young, married couple, two more angels, with whom he was living. The husband worked for an insurance company, and the wife was a housewife. They had three little kids.

They lived in an old Victorian house at the end of a tree-lined street. From the outside, it looked like a house straight out of *Lady and the Tramp*. On the inside, it looked like the Sears catalog. It was warm and homey, like nothing I'd ever experienced before.

The wife asked me to live with them and be a part of their family. At first, I said "No." However, when I woke up the next day, and my options were to go back to the bar or walk the dog in the cemetery, I thought maybe I would consider her offer. I went to live with this lovely family.

They were Evangelical Christians, and twice a week, they held Bible studies in their home. I joined in and liked to sit back and watch as they all interacted with each other. I liked to sing. We sang hymns, and I was the best singer in the group. That made me feel good. In my heart, though, I knew that I wasn't ready to live that kind of a squeaky-clean life. I lived there for two years. They were good to me.

My drinking was still bad before this. When I went there, I quit drinking. I have no idea why they ever let me near their kids. I wouldn't let someone like I was then near my kid. I don't know why they did. I'm grateful that hey did.

I cried every day for three months. I would clean their bathroom, and then I would cry until I had no more tears. The sadness of my life erupted out of my heart, and I couldn't contain it any longer. I cried for all of us. I cried for those who couldn't love. I cried for the pain that lived deep in me, for the terrified girl trapped deep inside.

In those two years, they thought that I was like them, a born-again Christian. I went through the motions, though it wasn't what I was called to. I went to their prayer meetings and listened, trying to get it, really trying. It wasn't that I was rejecting God. I just couldn't be the kind of Christian they wanted me to be.

While living with them, I went back to school and took care of the house and the kids.

Seeing Jack

During this time, I was still obsessed with Jack, and I think he was still obsessed with me. I would see his car following me from time to time. He would pull up at the corner and then drive away. I continued seeing him all through the spring of my first year of living with that family. I would go see him, and we would make love, and I would go back to their house. I was having a hard time with that because I was lying to them. I didn't feel good about it. And he was still a criminal.

And then the unthinkable happened. Jack got shot. On a holiday weekend, Jack and his buddy, in their infinite criminal wisdom, decided to rob the Brinks guys as they descended the escalator in a busy department store. Brinks guards walked into the store with guns in their hands. This was not a well-thought-out plan.

Jack approached the guards with a gun in his hand, and they shot him. He escaped. They found him in the hospital almost having bled out at home while his girlfriend, a nurse, and an accomplice, tried to stop the bleeding.

I was a wreck. Not only was he with someone else, he was more dead than alive and going back to jail. I spent the next few weeks at the hospital with him. He was completely withdrawn, and would hardly talk to me, completely para-noid and afraid of everyone as he sank deeper and deeper into fear and depression. It was sad and tragic. Not that he didn't deserve what he got. He committed armed robberies, for God's sake. Lots of them.

This guy was incredibly brilliant and totally crazy, as often is the case with brilliant people. Thus, began the rounds of me visiting him in the hospital, the county jail for months while he awaited trial, and, after his conviction, trips to the state prison.

I couldn't let go. I was devastated. I thought I loved him.

It took me five years to get over him. I swore off sex at that time because I thought sex was the problem. I couldn't see that it was my own fear and loathing, lack of emotional attachment to myself, and all the other things that were hanging me up.

I finished school, and in the spring of my last year, I drove with a friend through New Hampshire. He had gone to Dartmouth and wanted to show me the campus. As I drove through the campus, I got the distinct impression that I was supposed to go to school there. I applied and got in. Who knew that I had what it took to get into an Ivy League college? I was gobsmacked.

I had gone back to drinking in my senior year and was drinking all that summer at Dartmouth. I realized at the end of the summer that I was going to be back on the streets if I didn't quit. I had given up trying to quit and began wishing that I'd never started drinking. It was equally as effective as trying to quit, which is to say, not at all.

I had my last drink at the end of August in 1980. I found the local 12-step group, and I found the first place in my life where I felt I belonged. It was irresistible. I couldn't stay away.

Getting Sober Was Not Enough

Getting sober was not enough. God bless the 12 steps. They saved my life, and I have not had a drink since the day I arrived on the doorstep, beaten "into a state of reasonable-ness"[13] as it says in the literature. The steps gave me an unshakeable framework for building a good life. However, I continued to choose people who helped me create the same kind of stress that I knew. I was hooked on it.

I met my husband in the 12-step rooms. We got married, and I had a beautiful daughter. I remember a feeling that something amazing and wonderful was going to happen to me. That feeling lasted for several days. I soon found out I was pregnant. OMG! That was not my idea of something wonderful. Statistically speaking, I should have been an abusive, terrible mother. I was terrified. I decided that if I was going to do this, I was not going to blame my baby for coming into this world. I would not do to her what was done to me.

With great trepidation, I awaited her arrival. The moment I looked into her eyes, I fell deeply in love for the first time in my life. I had no clue how to be a mother. All alone with her in the soft light of the hospital room, I asked God to raise her and to show me what I needed to do. Together with assistance from the wonderful people who helped me get sober in the 12-step rooms, I watched as my angel grew into a beautiful person.

At thirty-four, watching my baby, I realized that I had been like her, an innocent. I saw that babies were born with clean

---

13. *Alcoholics Anonymous*, Alcoholics Anonymous World Services, Inc., Third Edition, 1983. P.48

souls and that I wasn't born a bad person. That same year, I read a book *The Drama of the Gifted Child*, by Alice Miller, a Swiss psychologist and psychoanalyst of Polish-Jewish origin, noted for her books on parental child abuse. That book made me understand what my parents had done to me. It took me quite a while to really grasp that they tormented me. I resisted the idea until I finally accepted the fact that they were cruel to me, and I didn't deserve it.

I followed that book with one by Scott Peck, *The People of the Lie*.[14] That book showed me just how horrible parents can be to their children. Narcissism at its best. Narcissistic parents use their children to meet their own sick needs. I finally had to believe it.

During this time, I was accepted into a doctoral program, and we moved so that I could go to school. My husband thought he married a blue-collar worker, a restaurant chef. After all hadn't he followed me to Paris where I was in cooking school? Wasn't I going to use that education? What he didn't know was that I had been working only to put myself through school. This high school educated dyslexic carpenter found himself married to a PhD in Medieval English with a focus on French Medieval literature. He never really came to terms with it. I kept trying to be true to my working-class roots, while working my way into the company of the highly educated.

On the outside, my husband and I looked like the ideal couple. We looked like we loved one another. We seldom fought or argued because we seldom talked to each other. When I was a wreck in early sobriety, we focused mainly on my issues. I was working hard to get better. Once I saw a path forward through the program, I was like a dog on a bone. When I was better, and we didn't have my recovery as a focus, our relationship seemed to die.

14. Peck, M. Scott. *People of the Lie: The Hope for Healing Human Evil*. Arrow Books, 2006.

I always looked like the crazy one. He always looked like a cool breeze. I became haranguing. He just laughed everything off. When we went to therapy at my behest, the therapists always ended up talking about me, and why I was such a wreck and how he wasn't. Can you say, "Gaslighting?"[15] He was quite good at getting me all spun up, and then he would stand back and smirk at me. He withheld so much from me. He was not physically attracted to me. And I tolerated it. I thought I was at fault. I thought that I had to put all the work into the relationship. He was OK with that. I think that is why he was with me.

I noticed in my own experience and watching other women. Weak men are attracted to strong women. We always seem to have an entourage waiting for us to take care of them. The problem is that I thought it was my job to take care of them.

Two incidences finally made me realize it was over. We had serious money problems. Neither of us was able to earn a good living.

The first final straw came when I had a car accident, and I hadn't paid the car insurance. The insurance grace period ended at 12:01 am the day of the accident. I was deemed at fault in the accident. I was so upset that I put us in such financial jeopardy. It was such an emotional experience that it changed me in a heartbeat.

There are two ways to change. One way is quickly in response to an extreme emotional experience. The second way is slowly over time through repetition. This was for me a pivotal emotional experience. I determined at that point that I was going to learn to earn more money. Someone told me about a 12-step program for debt and under-earning.

I found the program and learned that under-earning was a spiritual issue. Once I realized that, I knew what to do. I began

---

15. Gaslighting – manipulating (someone) by psychological means into questioning their own sanity.

working as hard as I could to make my financial situation better. My husband wouldn't. He finally said to me one day, "You do it. If you do it, it will work for both of us." Stunned, I felt like he had punched me in the stomach. For years, I strongly suspected that he was leaning on me, and finally, he came out and said it. In order to keep him, I had to work on my recovery AND HIS. Once again, I was in a position where I was responsible for someone else's life, just like when I was growing up. I was devastated to finally see it.

The second final straw came after yet one more conversation about our lack of physical intimacy. He looked at me and said, "Why don't you take a lover?" OMG. I was crushed. It was over. What kind of a husband says that to his wife? One that is not really a husband, that's who.

Our issues were just too much for us. I certainly didn't know what I needed or wanted. Neither of us was able to articulate what we needed. Maybe we didn't know either. He never told me that he didn't like something I was doing. He just grew more and more remote. I grew to believe that he didn't like me rather than not liking something I was doing. At the end, I think it was true that he just didn't like me. He called me an intensity junkie. He was right. I was hooked on it. What he could not see, and I did not know at the time, was that I was with him because he helped me create what I needed. I needed the stress, the fear, the emotional withholding, lack of physical intimacy, and anxiety because dealing with all that was what made me feel alive.

I was just trying to raise a kid the best I knew how. I lasted seventeen years in that marriage. Finally, the stress of it, the lack of physical intimacy, the withholding of affection, the stress over the lack of money, his fierce resentment of my education, and the exhaustion of trying to be the person I thought he wanted me to be took its toll on me. I collapsed with a serious stress-related illness. I was in bed for six months. When I got up, I realized the marriage had to be over or I was going to die. I finally was well enough to make him leave.

I lost most of our friends. Most of them took his side. After all, he wasn't the crazy one. They wondered how I could leave such a great guy.

Divorcing him saved my life, although it did not fix me. I continued to participate in relationships that recreated the experience I had in my family. I chose bullies for friends, egocentric people whom I allowed to dominate me.

I continued studying personal development and was making major strides in my financial recovery, although I was not letting go of the fear and anger at my family and shame at myself.[16]

At one of Tony Robbins' amazing events, I had an experience that freed me from the anger I held against my family. During a particularly powerful meditation led by an Indian mahatma, I could feel all the anger drain from me and I forgave my father. I was exhilarated; I was liberated; I felt totally free. Five days later, I plunged into the blackest depression I'd ever had. What I learned was right behind anger is depression. I was not to come out of it for nearly five years. Part of the reason it took so long to come out of it was because I was in another abusive relationship. After my husband, I had one short-lived relationship with a man whom I suspected had multiple personalities. I would leave the room and come back to a completely different person. That was weird. Then a six-year relationship with another abusive guy. Both were angry, narcissistic men.

The last man I was with for six years could be so sweet. He reminded me of my grandmother whom I loved so much. But he had a seething anger inside him that over shadowed any

16. *The Body Keeps the Score: Brain, Mind, and Body in the Healing of Trauma*, Van der Kolk, Bessel A. - Penguin Books – 2015. P.13

sweetness he might display at times. At any given moment he might erupt into a rage over seemingly insignificant things. I never knew what might cause these outbursts. The randomness of his anger kept me on constant high alert. He was controlling. He would comment on the least little thing I did. He commented on my handwriting, how much toilet paper I used. Really?!! Do you really want me to use less than what I need to do the job? He would tell me how to cook. I've cooked professionally for many years and studied cooking in Paris. Plus, I cooked for a family for twenty years. I think I've got this!!

He would burst out in a rage at the least thing. I never was able to identify what would trigger the explosion; I walked on eggshells all the time. He didn't like any of my friends; I thought I had to give them up and did. I watched as I hid parts of myself that would set him off. I was quite aware by this time of what I was doing. I had not yet learned that I didn't have to do it. I was still programmed to react rather than respond to people. At fifty, I did not yet have any sense of who I was. With him I became smaller and smaller until I no longer existed.

The hammer dropped one night when he was screaming at me one more time. I summoned the courage to say, "Stop shouting at me." He replied as loudly as he could, "I-AM-NOT-SHOUTING-AT-YOU!" That was it. I was done. I immediately grabbed my "go" bag and was out the door. I moved into my old apartment. It was another year and a half before I could finally leave him. Ultimately, I had to move away. I took the cats and moved to California. I told him I was not coming back. He finally let go.

On My Own at Last!

Two months later, when I got back from California, I entered a five-day program for codependency at a facility in Pennsylvania. Codependency is a learned behavior that can be passed down from one generation to another. It is an emotional and behavioral condition that affects an individual's ability to have a healthy, mutually satisfying relationship. It is also known as "relationship addiction" because people with codependency often form or maintain relationships that are one-sided, emotionally destructive and/or abusive.[17]

At the end of that program, they suggested that I go back into therapy yet one more time. I found someone highly recommended, who turned out to be crazier than I was. For six weeks, she sat and parroted back to me my words.

Me: "I was unhappy." **Her:** "You were unhappy."

Me: "I had to get away." **Her:** "You had to get away."

Me: "I don't understand what I'm doing wrong." **Her:** "You don't understand what you're doing wrong."

That went on for the entire hour for six visits. When I quit, she stalked me for weeks trying to get me to come back. Wow! A codependent, stalker therapist. That is not reassuring for the state of modern psychotherapy.

Next, I tried a man who wanted me to write a ten-page bio. When I told him that I did not want to do it, he said it would make his job easier. Wrong thing to say! I unloaded on him, "I don't give a fuck how much easier it makes your job. This is about ME!" I was starting to find my voice. Poor

17. Co-Dependency." Mental Health America, 8 Dec. 2016, www.mentalhealthamerica.net/co-dependency

man. He must have just thought I was crazy. He did not know that was a HUGE sign of recovery for me.

Most of the so-called therapists I encountered were at best incompetent and at worst damaging. Ashley Montagu, the well-known social anthropologist, once quipped: "A psychologist is a non-swimmer acting as a lifeguard."

MY TRAUMA RECOVERY
BEGINS IN EARNEST

A lovely woman I met in California advertised on Facebook for a course she was teaching from what I called "Airy-Fairy U." I signed up for it. My mind kept shouting at me, "What are you doing? You are going to try this New Age, woo-woo crap instead of real therapy? You really are nuts!" I derided myself for being so stupid.

It ended up being the best thing I could have done for myself. She turned out to be a brilliant life coach who has been able to help me more that anyone I have ever worked with.

She began by teaching me that everything is energy and vibration. We know this from the study of physics. Both Albert Einstein and Nicola Tesla said that everything in the universe vibrates with a frequency.

Einstein wrote, "Everything is energy, and that's all there is to it. Match the frequency of the reality you want, and you cannot help but get that reality. It can be no other way. This is not philosophy. This is physics."

Tesla wrote, "If you want to find the secrets of the universe, think in terms of energy, frequency, and vibration."

People vibrate at frequencies that we can change. The higher the signature of your frequency, the happier you will be. The high frequencies are love and joy, and the low frequencies are anger, fear, and depression. If you want to change the state of your mind, you must change the frequency on which your thoughts reside.

As I began to work with my energy signatures, and learned to raise my attitudes and beliefs from fear and anger to love and joy, I grew relatively quickly.

Your thoughts come from your beliefs. If they are mostly negative, it's because your beliefs are false and must be changed. Identifying faulty core beliefs is maybe the most important thing a person can do.

I learned about how my subconscious holds the instructions for how I want to live my life. These instructions were installed and updated continually from the day I was born. A baby's subconscious mind is wide open. The part of the brain, which filters information, has not developed yet in a newborn's brain. It takes a good twenty years for the brain to fully develop. A baby just absorbs into the subconscious whatever input is around it. The messages of the first two years of baby's life are important. If you abuse a baby from birth to age two, you will never really have a mentally healthy person without a strenuous effort of rebuilding the subconscious.

The information stored in the subconscious creates what we call paradigms. These paradigms are a multitude of beliefs and habits aggregated over the years from input from the five senses to the conscious mind, which sends them to the subconscious mind. These paradigms drive all our habitual behavior. And almost all our behavior is habitual.[18] The brain likes to automate our thinking. Electrical impulses through the brain take the path of least resistance. As the same thought takes the same path, that path becomes deeper, and the habit becomes stronger.

As your brain learns and grows, it changes shape to accommodate the new data. This is the good news. Scientists now know that the brain never stops changing and growing and repairing itself. This is called neuroplasticity.

---

18. http://www.proctorgallagherinstitute.com/events/paradigm-shift

To form a new habit, you must reinforce the path the new idea takes through the neural network.

If I want to change my behavior, I must first change the instructions in my subconscious mind. I can try all I want to raise my frequency; but if the frequency thermostat in my subconscious mind is set at depression, I may jump up to excitement or happiness, or any other higher frequency, however, my subconscious thermostat will always bring me back to depression.

The only way to change permanently is to change the paradigms in our subconscious mind. Our five senses created the paradigms. We took all the information coming into our mind. The way to change the paradigms is to install new paradigms.

Buckminster Fuller said, "You never change things by fighting the existing reality. To change something, build a new model that makes the existing model obsolete."

You can only change the old paradigm by creating a new one that renders the old way of thinking obsolete.

One night, when I was finally sick of the battle, I declared aloud to the empty room, "I'm going to live alone." As soon as I made the declaration, an overwhelming feeling of impending doom descended on me. It was as if all the voices of every person I had ever allowed to abuse me rose up as one, announcing that they were coming after me. "I do not care if it kills me," I screamed back at them. "It would be better to be dead than to go through another abusive relationship."

I decided at that moment that I was never going to allow anybody else to tell me who I was, who I could or could not be. I finally had enough.

Three Years Later

Everything in my life was great. I felt more positive and hopeful. I had a stronger sense of self; I was financially independent and making good money.

Then in September of 2012, the worst happened. I discovered that I had cancer – lymphoma – on my hipbones.

This is a perfect example of h how the subconscious works. There is a paradigm we hold in our subconscious mind of how we are going to live.

My subconscious mind was going to force me to continue to live according to the blueprint it had. Now that I was not going to choose bad relationships, it was going to find another way to keep me in fear. Fear was the message I was feeding it. It dished up fear for me in any way it could.

I know I didn't get sick by accident. I know now that if you do not live your true essence, you live in constant stress that puts a huge strain on your mind and body. Because of the stress caused by not being true to myself, I ended up with two serious illnesses. They were each a wake-up call to change direction and do things differently.

The cancer did not happen overnight. The doctors think I had had it for several years. Doctors think the cancer began in 2009. When I left that guy and went to California in November 2009, I was extremely fatigued with little energy for life. I thought I was just depressed or burned out from a stressful job and personal life. I used to walk at least three miles a day, and in my prime, it was up to five to ten miles a day. I found walking to be one of the best forms of exercise and a great way to clear my head and control emotions. Walking is also very egalitarian; unlike going to the gym, everybody can afford to walk! I was so beaten down and tired that I had stopped walking. And I began to experience the pain in my hip.

How Do We Change the Instructions in the Subconscious Mind?

I learned that I had to begin giving my subconscious new instructions for my life. I had to find a way to change the thinking patterns that were keeping me in fear. My coach was working hard to help me do just that.

You cannot change your life using the same thinking that got you where you are. I recently heard this on a TV drama. "Captivity is a mentality. It is a thing you carry with you."[19] I was captive to the prison I entered as a kid. Let me remind you at this point what I mentioned at the beginning. Traditional therapy does not work for traumatized people. Rehashing the stories, as you must in traditional talk therapy, only stirs up the brain to reproduce the feelings of the event, which we re-experience, sending us into a downward spiral until we are reliving the event as if it were happening to us in this moment.

Oh, great. Where does that leave me? Well, it is good news. Because now you have an opportunity to learn about the other thinking that is available to you – your higher faculties.

Most of us live on autopilot focusing on only what we perceive with our five senses – sight, hearing, touch, taste, and smell. We react to life based on what comes to us through these avenues. These senses are important, vital to our existence even. However, when you are trying to bust out of a lifetime of behaviors, these senses will not get you very far. They keep you firmly entrenched in what is happening before your eyes, and you keep getting more and more of what is happening before your eyes.

19. The OA, American Film Drama, Netflix.

WHAT YOU NEED ARE
SUPER POWERS!

I learned about these super powers through the material of Bob Proctor and Sandy Gallagher. Bob and Sandy call them the higher faculties. I call them super powers. We all have super powers at our control. With these super powers, we can change into whomever we want to become. "Where are my super powers?" you might ask. These super powers are – Imagination, Intuition, Perception, Will, Memory, and Reason. Very few people are taught about these powers, and we are often even scolded for using them. For example, imagination – daydreaming – how many times as a kid did your parents and teachers scold you for daydreaming, for wasting time? Imagination is a huge requirement for changing your life. If you do not dream or a have a vision of what your life could be like, or what you would like your life to be, there is no roadmap out of your current situation. Your dreams and visions are your roadmap, or at least they give you a destination to aim for.

Let's examine these faculties.

The Super Power
Imagination

Your subconscious mind does not know the difference between an imagined event and a real one. If you do not believe me, think of the last time you had a vivid, happy dream or a nightmare that scared you. You awoke from that dream either with wonderful feelings, or you awoke with a racing heart and were filled with fear. Nothing actually happened to you. But your subconscious reacted as though the dreamed events really happened, causing a physical response. You either felt great or had the fight or flight response.

I first read *The Lord of the Rings* trilogy when I was much younger. The day I read the part where Gandalf "died" in the mines of Moria, I was crushed. The death of this fictitious person devastated me. That was an imaginary event, however, my subconscious mind didn't know it. I reacted as though I had lost a real friend. I felt grief all day.

My imagination was so hooked into the story that I couldn't tell the difference between a character in a book and a real human being. Our imaginations are that powerful. However, most of the time, we use it to scare the shit out of ourselves.

Using your higher faculties, you can begin to feed your subconscious mind new operating instructions for how your life should look. Yes, you can start to program your own mind to change its behavior.

"But I don't have a very good imagination!" At first, it may seem that way. Part of the problem for traumatized people is that our imaginations have been impaired.[20] We often cannot see beyond the trauma, or we see everything in our life through the lens of that trauma. But is this trauma not part of the imagination? Except that you are imagining the

---

20. *The Body Keeps the Score: Brain, Mind, and Body in the Healing of Trauma*, Van der Kolk, Bessel A. – Penguin Books – 2015. P17

old trauma replaying. We are using our imaginations to harm us.

How do you break out of the box?

Everything that exists began in the imagination. Before anything is manifested on the material plane, it is first created in the imagination. The "thing" began with an idea. Let's take a house, for example. Someone has an idea for a building. Someone writes down the idea as in the blueprints for a building. The builder reads those plans and creates the building with hard materials. In this way, all ideas go from unmanifested energy to manifested energy in material form.

We begin with the idea. We breathe life into it with our repetition and emotional engagement, we begin to make plans, we study, learn, and discover ways to make it happen. We act on those ways and finally, it appears in our life. Remember what Einstein said, "Match the frequency of the reality you want, and you cannot help but get that reality." As you apply yourself to imagining what you want, putting all your emotion behind it, studying and learning everything you can about it, and not deviating from that desire, you are raising your frequency to match the frequency of the thing you want. When you declare to God, or the universal intelligence, what you want and deepen the desire by creating a new subconscious paradigm, God begins to move those things to you. "Faith is the substance of things hoped for, the evidence of things not seen."[21] You must believe it before you can see it.

YOUR IMAGINATION CAN COMMUNICATE WITH YOU!

Communication with your imagination is a two-way street. You can use your will to direct it, and it can give you information through dreams or visions. My subconscious mind gave me all kinds of visions and imaginings.

21. Hebrews 11:1.

A series of visions gave me information about myself. I couldn't always interpret what the information was in real time. Often it was years before I knew what the visions meant. The messages from these visions in my imagination kept me going.

The Cave Vision

I began to have a serial vision over about a twenty-year period. I don't remember when I started seeing this vision. It just appeared to me at odd times in images flashing on my mind. Sometimes I would daydream it. I know now that it chronicled the deepening understanding I was gathering about my spiritual captivity and increasing freedom from spiritual and psychological bondage.

The vision started with me standing in front of a big rock. The vision would flash into my mind. I would see myself standing in front of a huge boulder that was many feet taller than me. This came to me during a time when I was lost. My soul was as dense as rock, and I had no spiritual vision. This was during the darkest time of my life, and my drinking was at its worst.

After a long while, the vision showed me the rock had a door that was open just a crack. I just stood in front of the door. Then one day, after a long time of the door being open just a crack, I saw that the door was wide open; and over the course of time, I slowly made my way down the stairs that appeared one at a time carved into the rock.

After another long period, I walked all the way down to the landing at the bottom of the stairs. I stood on the landing, terrified to do anything or to see what else was there. Another stretch of time passed, and then one day in the vision I turned the corner into a large, empty, stoned-walled room like in a medieval castle.

Then a bench appeared, and then an old woman clothed in a hooded cloak appeared sitting on the bench. I eventually sat by her with my head on her lap. She just sat there allowing me to be near her. I think this represented me becoming more attached to the world of people.

I eventually stood up from sitting with the old woman and found a door in the room. These episodes were taking place over broad expanses of time. It might have been a year or more between any change in the events in the vision.

I eventually saw myself opening the door, which led to a stairway that sparkled with a soft golden light illuminating the walls that looked like a bright pinkish golden geode. Once I made my way down those stairs, I found another room.

After a while, I turned and discovered a column of pure energy that shot up out of a hole in the floor of the room. It shot upward like water from a fire hydrant. It was powerful and dangerous looking. One morning I was sitting in church, a rare occurrence for me, when suddenly my vision appeared to me, and I was standing in front of the pillar of energy. I suddenly thrust my arm into the energy. I was exhilarated. I kept my arm there and, after another long while, I climbed into the energy. Finally, the roof opened, and I flew out into the sunshine and fresh air.

The vision seemed to be complete. I haven't had another episode appear to me in many years. I now know that it symbolized the various stages of my spiritual growth and my ability to reach the deepest part of myself and be energized by Source Energy – what I call God, which gave me the ability to fly to freedom.

How to Direct Your Imagination

Begin Telling a New Story!

New Age philosophy taught me the principle of telling a story the way you want it and not repeating the story of what happened. The story of what happened is what you perceived with your five senses. Remember that we are now focusing on our super powers. The super power of imagination showed me that I could tell a different story. Some people call this "reframing."

Practicing telling a different story breaks the old thought patterns. A belief is just a thought that you repeat often enough until you finally believe it. One of the biggest beliefs I had was that my parents were bad people. It is true that they did bad things to me. And I don't want to hear that old chestnut, "They did the best they could." What these people did to me is no one's best. I now can say they did ALL they could, but certainly not the BEST they could. When someone does their best, they are putting effort into an activity. Saying that to a traumatized person is the same as telling them they don't have the right to the experience of their pain. It is one more way of denying their authenticity. Someone harmed you. That is a fact.

But to heal, I had to find another story to tell myself because the story of my family being bad people was hurting me and holding me in a pattern of suffering.

I read, and this is probably a poor representation of what the Buddhists believe, that there is a Buddhist principle that our souls make plans with each other on the immaterial plane about what we are going to learn together on the material plane. We move to the material plane and live out the events we need to perform so that we all learn the lessons we planned.

I have no idea if this is true or even if I understood it correctly. The thought took hold in my mind that my soul and the souls of my parents agreed that I was going to learn compassion and kindness by experiencing abuse. They agreed to live their lives on this plane in this lifetime as unhappy, mean people so that I could learn these lessons. Using that scenario, the story I now tell is that my parents sacrificed their lives for me so that I could learn the lessons I needed.

Did this actually happen? Who knows? But telling myself this new story cracked open the old story that kept me stuck in pain and suffering. I was able to reframe it so that I could begin to experience love for them. The new story allows me to engage the possibility that they loved me even a little, and eventually, I was able to think that they gave up a lot for me – that they sacrificed their lives for me. The pain and suffering left me. I began to feel love for them. I WILL NEVER LIKE WHAT THEY DID TO ME! And you don't have to either. But if I want to live without resentment, fear, and suffering, I need to view the situation from another point of view.

I was able, using my imagination, to at least engage the possibility of another point of view.

∽

EXERCISE

What is a story you need to change?

Write the story, briefly so as not to trigger any stress. Now using your imagination, think of a way to tell a better story about what happened to you. What lesson did you learn from the bad experience? How can you use that experience to deepen your spiritual growth?

Write the new story. How does that make you feel? Do you feel more powerful, or does it make you feel powerless? If you feel less powerful, discard that story. Write the story in a way that makes you feel good about yourself, makes you feel like a powerhouse. Underneath all the chaos, we are perfect and whole. Our spiritual DNA is perfect. Let yourself sink beneath the chaos to the foundation of your being, which is perfect. The new story can take you there.

THE SUPER POWER
WILL

Will gives me the ability to hold one idea in my mind long enough to give me direction. Using my will, I forced myself to tell a different story about my life. I can use my will to keep my attention focused on things that support my spiritual and mental health.

We often use our will power to keep us stuck in fear, anger, and suffering. Somewhere in the AA literature, it says that aligning our will with the will of God is the proper use of will power. If I take that to mean that aligning my will with the forces that will support my spiritual growth, that will help create a healthy mind, I can use my willpower to tell positive stories that lead me into higher and higher frequencies.

The higher frequencies are love and joy. The lower frequencies are anger and fear.

Here is a brief story of how I used my will to help me. I had a horrible fear of the dentist. As a kid, I ate a lot of sugar, and I had the dental caries to prove it. Sometimes I would have as many as fifteen cavities the dentist had to fill at one time. It was horrifying. When I got older and went to the dentist on my own, he told me that if I flossed my teeth every day, I would never get another cavity in my teeth. I was thrilled to think I would never have to go through the pain of a filling again. Off I went, floss in hand, toward a new life free of scary dental work.

The next day when I had to floss my teeth, my subconscious mind had another idea. It was not going to allow me to floss my teeth. I just couldn't make myself do it. One day went by without it, then a second day. By the third day, the fear of the dentist's drill got to me, though I still couldn't make myself floss.

This is how I used my will to make me floss.

I said to myself, "OK, you don't have to floss, but you cannot get up out of this chair until you do." I was extremely active and quite agitated back then, so sitting down alone with no music or any distraction was quite difficult for me. Five minutes went by. Ten minutes went by. Finally, after about twenty minutes, I gave in and flossed my teeth. I had to do this exercise every day in decreasing amounts of time for about a month. One day I missed flossing my teeth; and when I woke up the next day, my teeth felt so yucky, I couldn't wait to floss. In more than forty years, I have probably only skipped flossing my teeth about ten times. Each day I cannot wait to floss because the feeling of not flossing is so horrible. It doesn't matter how sick or crappy I feel; I floss every day.

And I have never had another cavity in my teeth.

Your will is a powerful ally in helping you heal. You are not broken. You are only distracted by the anguish that affected your brain. You can use this higher faculty to lead you from pain to freedom. My coach says to me often, "You have to get smarter than your brain." What is your reason for wanting to change? Allow that to draw you toward the goal.

~

EXERCISE

Now that you have written a new story about your life, read this story twice a day for ninety days. Your mind will balk at this.

Use your will and the enticement of a happier life to lead you on.

I used fear to spur me on. That works. But if you can have a goal with a higher frequency, that will be all the better. Use increased happiness to draw you on. We will do everything we can to avoid pain and obtain pleasure. Use that human tendency to further your best interest.

As you read your story daily, you may find it changes. Add to your story as you discover things you want in your life. Make sure you are the star of your story. This is YOUR life. No one has the right to take that from you.

The Super Power Perception

Perception is the way you see something. It's your point of view. As I discussed, I had to reframe the way I perceived my situation growing up to allow my attitudes to change. It is not easy to give up one's way of thinking. However, it is worth the effort. Allow your misery to drive you to find another way. Being miserable is only good if you use it for motivation to change. When the fear of the unknown is outweighed by the misery you feel, you will change. When the pain is great enough, you will change.

~

Exercise

Think of a situation that is fearful to you. You are afraid of this situation because of your point of view.

Put yourself in the position of a very confident person. How would this person perceive the situation? If you cannot do this, find a confident person and ask them how they handle this situation.

Can you begin to look at it from that point of view?

THE SUPER POWER REASON

I always used to tell myself that I was a bad person. What I did was use my super power "Reason" to determine if I was, in fact, a bad person. I began by making a list of all the bad people I could think of.

My list began with Adolf Hitler, Jeffrey Dahmer, and Charles Manson. OK, I am not a monomaniacal, mass murdering cannibal. That is a good start.

Next on my list: Bernie Madoff, Michael Milken, Jeffrey Skilling of the Enron debacle. OK, I am not a corporate thief bilking millions of people out of money.

Next list: everyone who was ever mean to me. OK, I am not a bully. I might be a milquetoast, but I am not a bully. I do not try to push people into doing what I want.

Then I made a list of all the people I admire, which included most of the schoolteachers I really liked and who helped me; I included Jesus, Buddha, and the Dalai Lama. I included Albert Einstein and Albert Schweitzer. My best friend from grade school, CarolAnn, was on that list. She was the best person I knew as a kid. Gandalf the wizard was on the list. Nancy Drew and Cordelia, the daughter of King Lear, were on the list. I realized that I admire good people, and I have a heart that wants people to be happy and succeed.

Have I done things I am not proud of? Yes! I am a human being who did things I should not have done. I am not inherently a bad person.

I had to let go of the guilt I felt for the things I had done wrong. I had a tool from the 12 steps that worked well. I made a searching and fearless inventory, and I admitted to God, myself, and another human being the exact nature of my wrongs. Next, I went made amends for the wrongs I did to people. I relieved my guilty conscience by owning up to what I did wrong, not focusing on what the other person did at all. I liberated myself from the guilt and shame I experienced. I could finally let go of it.

Having grown up with a family who never believed in forgiveness, I had to learn what forgiveness is and cultivate it within me. Forgiving myself is the hardest to manage.

But my reasoning abilities allowed me to help myself out of darkness into the light of the truth about me.

∽

Exercise

Identify one thought pattern that is keeping you from living fully. Using your reasoning abilities, what can you do to improve your situation? Can you identify the thoughts that are holding you back?

Make a list of the thoughts. Now write a list of thoughts that would serve you better. Using your higher faculty of will, practice those thoughts for a week. At the end of the week, write the situation as you now see it. Has it improved?

The Super Power Intuition

A favorite technique of abusers the world over is "gaslighting." Gaslighting is a form of manipulation that casts doubt in the mind of a person designed to make them question their own intuition and even their own sanity. Using persistent denial, contradiction, and lying, the gaslighter destabilizes a person's belief in what they see and feel.

My family taught me that what I thought, felt, and knew were wrong. I learned to distrust my thinking, feelings, and intelligence at an early age. When I told my mother not to tell lies, she hissed at me, "I don't lie. Don't ever say that I lie." I knew that she lied and learned not to say it again. It didn't matter what I thought; they told me, either by word or deed, that I didn't get it right. Only what they wanted me to believe was correct.

On a conscious level, I believed that I was wrong, bad, stupid, etc. On an unconscious level, I knew differently. This knowledge couldn't come to the surface during waking hours. After I went to sleep, though, the truth spoke to me in the form of a nightmare. From an early age, I had a recurring nightmare that scared the hell out of me. It is inconsequential what the actual events were in the dream, but it was always the same.

My imagination was telling me that I knew what was going on in the family. My conscious mind fought against the truth, and the dissonance terrified me.

I had that dream until I taught myself to wake myself up from it by pressing my forehead against the bookshelf at the head of my bed. Once I started preventing myself from facing the truth in my dreams, I began overeating. It took me until I was forty-five-years old in graduate school and working with a brilliant therapist who helped me unravel the dream, to know that the dream was telling me, what I knew to be true. The fear resulted because I wasn't allowed to speak the truth. My intuition would not allow itself to be thwarted. If I wouldn't acknowledge it in the daylight when I was conscious, it was going to come out when I was asleep. If I refused to let it come to me in my sleep, it was going to annoy the crap out of me with a aberrant behavior like over eating.

Support from a trusted coach and relationships with strong women, I was able to see that I knew the truth. It was a much longer time before I put myself into a situation where I was able to speak the truth. Cutting out of my life anyone who did not allow me to speak the truth took longer. But now I am free to speak the truth. If anyone doesn't like it… too frickin' bad.

The Super Power Memory

The memories of traumatized people are not our friends. We often wish we could have amnesia so as not to remember what happened. I freed myself from my memories with a technique that came to me in a flash of inspiration one day.

This is a technique I was given in a vision that has helped me break open old memories releasing their grip on me. In this technique, the memory comes to mind and begins to trigger me. But I use my will to stop the action of the memory. I use stop action like a scene in a movie where everyone freezes except for one person. All the characters freeze. In my mind, I step into the scene as I am today, a confident, powerful woman. My parents, me as a child, and my sisters, whomever is in the memory, are frozen, and I take charge of the situation. I take my mother by the shoulders and move her out of the picture. I grab my father's arm as he is about to hit my sister and shove him away from her. I then pick up all the children, wipe their tears, clean their faces, hold and comfort them. I promise to take good care of the kids never letting anyone hurt them ever again.

This was and still is a powerful tool that I employed. I used this for every memory that triggered a post-traumatic flashback. One by one, I was able to defuse the energy that kept me regressing into the child I was during those events. I continue to find memories that I haven't healed yet. Earlier today, as I write this, a persistent memory arose from early childhood. It has haunted me. Today I became aware that I could use this technique on it. For the first time since the day it happened, I am not wracked with guilt over it.

~

Exercise

The next time a bad memory comes to mind, remind yourself to become an observer of the memory instead of a participant in the action. Practice stopping the action of the memory as soon as you can. Let the scene freeze. See yourself as you are today, not as the participant in the past, but as you are today a grown person with authority, stepping into the scene. How can you change the action of the scene?

This may take some time to master because it is not always easy for me to see that I am lost in the memory. Once I am aware, I can begin to take control.

OTHER TECHNIQUES I USED TO HELP FREE MYSELF!

FIND A CHAMPION!

I cannot emphasize enough how important it is for me to have a mentor. I use a Transformational Coach. There are all kinds of coaches for business and sports. I found one that helped me transform my life. I need someone I trust completely, whom I know without a doubt has no agenda for me beyond my health and happiness, that I can rely on to help me through this labyrinth of life. I work with a coach weekly.

Life coaching is a profession that is belittled in the mainstream media. On the new *Roseanne* show, Jackie, the wacko, pink-hat-wearing, following-every-trend-there-is, crazy sister, is a life coach.

Do not be fooled. Coaching is way better than psychotherapy for those of us who are traumatized. Therapy focuses attention on what happened causing us to spiral back into the trauma. Coaching focuses your attention on what you want in life, not what happened to you in the past. We all have strengths and weaknesses. The traumatized person is hyper-focused on the trauma. A coach can help you focus your thoughts away from the trauma onto your strengths, so you can begin to access the power you possess.

A coach helps you identify words and phrases you are using against yourself and can help you begin to talk about yourself in positive ways that build belief in how powerful you can be. In many ways, it is easier to be weak than strong.

A quote attributed to Marianne Williamson[22] says, "Our deepest fear is not that we are inadequate, our deepest fear is that we are powerful beyond measure. It is our light, not our darkness that frightens us."

There is much to be said for weakness. It feels like the easier way. We don't have to show up and fight for ourselves. We can take the easy way out. What a criminal waste of a life.

A coach can hold you accountable and ease you into doing the difficult work of building yourself into an amazing person.

We live in a holistic universe. This means that everything that exists is available to everyone all the time. Everything that is available to Bill Gates or Albert Einstein is available to you. All the words that Shakespeare used are available to you. All the ideas that exist are there for you to draw to yourself.

All the energy of the universe is available to you any time you open yourself to it.

A coach can help you become the person you are meant to become. The only limits are the ones that we place on ourselves.

Ask Yourself, "Does this Make Me Feel Powerful or Powerless?"

This is a powerful question. When you are about to do something or become aware of a thought, ask yourself, "Does this make me feel powerful or powerless?" Powerless feels weak, maybe painful in your body, unhappy, maybe depressed. Powerful makes you feel good, strong, happy, and maybe even joyful.

If you are about to do something, and it doesn't make you feel powerful, don't do it. Don't ever act or choose until you feel powerful.

22. Marianne Williamson is an American spiritual teacher, author, and lecturer. She has published twelve books, including four *New York Times* number one best-sellers.

FORGIVENESS

Forgiving myself did not come easily. I lived with unrelenting condemnation, so forgiveness was foreign to me. I had to begin to let myself off the hook.

This is what I did to forgive myself: I was extremely judgmental of other people. Feeling badly toward someone else is generally a reflection of something we dislike about ourselves. Each time I find myself judging myself or someone else, I put my hand over my heart and repeat, "I forgive myself for judging myself as X." I do that as many times as I need to until I have let go of that bad feeling. Sometimes I know why I am angry with myself, and sometimes I do not. I do not need to know. I just need to identify the judgment and forgive myself for holding it.

Another thing I do when I realize that I am judging someone is just to acknowledge that I am judging. I repeat, "You are judging her, you are judging, you are judging." Just the acknowledging, without recrimination to myself, allowed me to let go of the habit. As I felt better about myself, I could feel better toward others. Loving myself is the prerequisite to loving others. I cannot give what I don't have. If I don't have love and forgiveness for me, I cannot love and forgive anyone else.

When I look at who I am today and what I want for other people, I can admit that I am a nice person and a good person. I can let myself off the hook for being human.

FIGURING OUT WHAT YOU WANT!

Getting clear on what you want is key. I did not know what I liked or what I wanted. One of the things I did to overcome this trait was to notice when I was feeling good about something. The George Washington Parkway is a beautiful road that runs along the Potomac River between Alexandria, VA, and Mount Vernon, the home of George Washington. One day when I did not feel good, I remembered how much I loved that road. I drove on that road just to get that good feeling. It was something I learned I could do to make myself feel better. During the time I was waiting for a diagnosis for what they thought was potentially deadly bone marrow cancer, and the actual diagnosis of a treatable cancer, I drove up and down that road several times a day because it gave me a sense of peace. I had learned I could do something on my own to make me feel better rather than turning to people for help that they were not able or supposed to give me. Sometimes the only person who can help me is me.

I began to get glimpses of what I wanted in my life. I wrote them down. My imagination began to stir and then kick into a higher gear.

Once I began to have an idea of what I wanted, I could write a life script. This script consisted of what I wanted my life to look like - how much money I wanted to earn, where I want to live, where I want to work.

My script looked something like this: I have confidence. I trust myself to do what is right for me. I respect myself. I speak kindly to myself. I have relationships with people who respect me and are kind and loving to me. I earn more than enough money to be fully self-supporting. I have a thriving business. I take at least one vacation a year. I live in a lovely home with two bedrooms and a balcony. I live in a safe part of town. I view all obstacles as challenges that help me grow.

Notice how I only use positive words. I don't write the negative. For example, "I don't want to be in debt." This is an ineffective approach because the subconscious won't hear the "I don't want to" part. It only understands "debt," and that is what it will produce. The better approach is to write and say, "I have a surplus of money at the end of each month. I have more than enough money to live on." My script is evolving. As I get stronger and can imagine more and more, my script has bigger and bigger dreams in it. The script you write can have anything in it as long as it is what you really want.

I create new scripts of my life as the old scripts are achieved. I continue to inform my subconscious about new directions I want to take. My subconscious takes the information and gives me the opportunities to grow.

You do not have to know how to get the things in your script; you only must get clear on what you want. Getting clear is the key. You have to know you want it and that you will do anything legal and moral to get it. That is not to say it will not work for illegal and immoral things because it will. I do not want the backlash that goes along with those illegal and immoral. I only just figured out I am a good person; I do not want to muddy those waters.

Faith is a muscle that you must use to get strong. Hebrews 11:1 in the Bible reads: "Now faith is the substance of things hoped for, the evidence of things not seen." If you want to change, you must believe it before you see it. You need to read your script until you can begin to believe it. Visualize yourself acting like the person you want to be. What does she wear? How long or short is her hair? How often does she get her hair and nails done? How does she speak to her children?

Read these characteristics and feel them. This should be a fun exercise because it is about how you want to feel and act. Let yourself feel it in your body. Move around, dance, get excited about the person you want to be. The movement will help deepen the experience in your subconscious mind.

You will fall back into old behavior from time to time. Relax. Don't fight it, but don't let yourself live there for very long. As soon as you can, pick up your script, and begin to read it again. Read it at least twice a day; more is better. Let yourself change. Let go of the old story. It doesn't serve you. Watch as you change and reward yourself for your positive behaviors.

We Should All Earn Lots of Money!

Earning more than enough money was a major tool to extricate me from fear. Everyone, particularly women and girls, should have a dream of becoming fully financially self-supporting.

> Wallace Wattles, in *The Science of Getting Rich*, writes: "Whatever may be said in praise of poverty, the fact remains that it is not possible to live a really complete or successful life unless one is rich. No man can rise to his greatest possible height in talent or soul development unless he has plenty of money; for to unfold the soul and to develop talent he must have many things to use, and he cannot have these things unless he has money to buy them with."

We should each be able to live our lives as independent, free agents. There is nothing more disempowering as not having enough money. Anyone who tells you it is spiritual to be poor has an agenda that is not in alignment with your highest good. You cannot be safe, have a strong connection to God, or help anyone, including yourself, when you do not have enough money to survive and to thrive. I know this from experience. I was poor most of my life, and now I have more than enough money to live on. I will choose wealthy over poor all day long.

If the women's movement really wants equality for women, we should teach our daughters how to produce wealth on their own. Women will only be free when we have real wealth – free to raise our children without having to be dependent on anyone else, if that is what we need to do. It blows my mind that when I tell women that I make more money than most of the men I work with, not one of them has ever asked me how I did it. It is equally important for young men to have lofty goals and to work hard to achieve them so as to be financially independent and successful. As parents, we do our children a great service by teaching them to reach for the stars.

Someone once said to me, "Do you want the bad guys to have all the money and therefore all the power? If you want to outdo the bad guys, you will have to have more money and therefore more power than them."

So Where Do You Start?

Everything begins with a decision. A decision is nothing more than determining that you are going to do only those things required to attain X. Think about the last time you wanted to see a movie. You looked on the internet for all the shows available. You sorted through until you saw the one you thought looked good and chose that one. All other information became irrelevant at that point. If you don't choose a movie to see, you will either stay home or stand in the lobby of the theater dithering over what to see.

Deciding means that you have cut off all avenues to anything else. When I decided to get wealthy, I didn't do anything that didn't further my goal. I haven't cleaned my own house in many years because it is a waste of my time. I would be the highest paid housekeeper in the history of the world. I get someone else to do it so that I can focus my attention on my mission.

This is how and when clearly deciding worked for me. In 1995 before the divorce, I met a young man who was a coach. He wanted me to get into this network marketing company. He coached me in prosperity thinking, which I now teach. He worked with me hard. When my marriage blew up, he coached me through it the best he could. I learned much from him about taking charge, becoming bigger than your problems, and stating what you want instead of focusing on what you see. I never made it in his network marketing company, but he helped me a lot.

Single mothers have an especially difficult time. After the divorce, I realized that I could not raise my teen-aged daughter on the money I was making – $35,000 a year in suburban DC, one of the most expensive places to live in the country. One night, recognizing what I needed to earn in order to do more than survive, I said out loud, "I need to make at least $100,000 a year." That declaration drew to me a series of events, which provided an avenue for me to increase my income. I began to see opportunities I had never seen previously.

> "*Where there is no way, God will provide a way*"
> ~ Michael Beckwith

My Reticular Activation System brought to my attention opportunities that had been there all along. I never saw how they could benefit me until I decided to make 100K a year. The desperation I felt provided the courage to propel me into action.

I saw an opportunity and approached the owner of another company with it. I bargained with him – hire me and pay me $65,000 (which at the time seemed like all the money in the world), and I will hook you up with this opportunity. He agreed, and I got the job, at the price I asked.

More opportunities started to arise that I boldly acted on, and within two years, I was making $90,000 with benefits. I went on from there to earn well over six figures.

It was amazing. Just by getting clear on what I needed, my subconscious mind was able to serve up things I could not see before. My courage, fueled by desperation, rose up and enabled me to take chances I never could take before. It is not spooky, woo-woo stuff. It's physics. When you give your subconscious mind a clearly defined order, it sorts through the myriad of data points surrounding you and only focuses on what you need to attain that goal. It is a brain thing.

Take Action!

Do something every day toward your goals. My good friend Phil Black, an amazing Transformational Coach, says, "Ordinary actions taken consistently over time lead to extraordinary results!" Nothing you do toward your goal is too small. Just make sure you take at least one step toward your goal every day. Make it a big step. That's how I wrote this book. About an hour a day, every day, and soon I had a book.

What Do You Need to Change?

Identify the behaviors that are holding you back. You can do this for everything you want to change. Choose one troubling situation after the next and write out the situation in excruciating detail. Write everything that you are doing. How are you reacting to events and people? What are the results you are getting? Read it again and circle all the behaviors that are not working.

Circle self-deprecatory phrases like, "I am overwhelmed," "I feel stupid and scared," "I doubt myself."

Rewrite the situation in the way you want to see it unfold. Write phrases like, "I confidently speak the truth," "I am excited to begin to…," "I eagerly create…," and "It is my great pleasure." If you have trouble with these phrases, put this phrase in front of them, "I look forward to being able to…" or "I look forward to being eager to create." These phrases, "I look forward to," or "Won't it be great when I can?…," short-circuit the mind's ability to argue with you.

Your subconscious will fight you at first because it is operating on old instructions. It wants to do what you ask of it. Today's behavior is based on instructions you gave your subconscious previously. As you give it the same clear instructions repeatedly, it will begin to present to you the opportunities to live into your script. It doesn't take as long as you think it will. It generally takes longer than you want it to. Use your super power of Will to continue the practice until you succeed.

You are in charge. That is the blessing of taking 100% responsibility for your life. You are in charge. You have always been in charge. You just didn't know how to use your super powers. No more being the victim. Now you are the boss. Be the kind of boss you have always wanted.

Once you are comfortable with the new phrases, write out the situation the way you want to see it unfold. This sounds simple, but it is powerful. This is the way that you overwrite the old paradigms and give the subconscious mind new operating instructions. It does not work simply to say, "I'm not going to do X anymore." You must keep repeating the new instructions, creating the image for the subconscious until you have created new neural pathways. It will feel uncomfortable, even perhaps terrifying, to change. Your ability to withstand that discomfort will be in proportion to the pain you have in the old life and the strength of the image you have for your future. Keep pushing yourself to repeat the new. It will, must, change when your energetic frequency aligns with the new behaviors.

You can also burn the list of ineffective behaviors to send a message to your subconscious mind. You are not doing this anymore. You want something different.

Read your script daily. Visualize yourself doing the new behaviors. You can do this with any new things you want to bring into your life.

You must be as relentless as a little kid if you are going to get what you want. If your mind denies you through one avenue, take another road into it. You must never give up until you have what you want.

Many of us heard "no" so many times that we think God, or Universe Intelligence, is going to say the same thing to us. God, or Universe Intelligence, is not like the petit people we have been dealing with. God, or the big UI, wants you to have everything you need to grow into the biggest and best version of yourself. Your expectation is what is going to slow things down. If you are expecting the old results, those are what you are going to get. You might want to say, "I expect great things to come into my life." "I anticipate having all the things I need to live life at the highest level."

Sometimes in response to some powerful emotional event, you might change in the twinkling of any eye. Although most change requires continual spaced repetition of the new instructions.

Remember that you are not focusing on your five senses anymore. They are doing the daily chores; for this huge life change, you are using your super powers, the higher faculties.

What are they again? Intuition, perception, will, memory, imagination, and reason. These tools will begin to shift you out of the old way of thinking and over the rainbow where your dreams really do come true.

You will not believe me. Your mind is already giving you all the reasons this won't work for you. That is only the old paradigm saying, "Wait a second. That is not the game plan." You will have to be firm and dedicated. Be relentless. The mind will shift. I suggest having an accountability partner or coach who knows about this stuff.

You can do this with any situation you want to change. The Law of Vibration is the primary law of the Universe. All things are energy that vibrates at a certain frequency. When you change the setting on the radio from 90.9 FM to 103.5 FM, you get a different radio station. The radio frequency assigned to each radio station is different from all others.

They send out their signal on their frequency. It is not possible to dial into 103.5 Classical station and get the Hip Hop programming on 90.9. You can only get what is playing on 90.9.

Your current frequency is bringing you all the things in your life that you have now. If you want things on another frequency, you must change your frequency, change the setting on your receiver, to bring it up to the frequency of the things you want yet do not have right now. Simple but not necessarily easy; it requires diligence and effort.

I know this may sound a bit ridiculous to those who haven't studied it and put it to the test. But I assure you that this is exactly what many have done to make major strides in removing bullies from their lives and becoming people who do not allow themselves to be abused. Anyone who stands in the way of self-growth doesn't get to stick around. They either move away from us voluntarily or are invited to leave by the new and improved, confident, stand-up-for-ourselves people that we have become!

REPETITION IS KEY

Diligence in sending the new message to the mind is essential. Repetition is the mother of all learning. You must continuously condition the mind to the new paradigm. You can do this with affirmations, with written goals, with images, or with sticky notes stuck all over your house. (You don't have to use sticky notes. If it creates too much clutter for you, use written goals.)

WRITTEN GOALS

Identify in your story what you want in your life. Make a list, write it out by hand, and read it out loud twice a day. Writing by hand and reading out loud involve different parts of the brain in this activity, reinforcing it more strongly in your mind. Moving your body while you are doing it adds another dimension, helping it to take hold strongly in your mind.

Vision Board

One of the ways to use repetition is to make a vision board. You can put on a poster or a PowerPoint slide deck all the things you want in your life. Most of the dreams that people imprint on vision boards come to pass. I heard this story about a guy who put a picture of a certain pickup truck on his vision board. The day the truck arrived, a kitten showed up on his front porch. When he looked at the picture of his truck, he saw that there was a kitten on the running board. OK, that is a little woo-woo.

Practice Daily Affirmations

Mainstream media has belittled affirmations to the point that it can be just plain embarrassing to tell people you use them. Cue *Saturday Night Live*'s Stuart Smalley[23]: "I'm good enough, I'm smart enough, and doggone it, people like me." He made us think that only weenie losers use affirmations.

But aren't we are using affirmations every day? Yes, however, mostly we are using them in the negative. "I'm such an idiot." "I'm so fat." "I have no friends." "I'm broke." "I'm scared." These are all affirmations that keep us stuck in faulty thinking.

My coach says you must get smarter than your brain. If you are going to talk to yourself, why not speak to yourself kindly and encouragingly? Give yourself a break. Aren't you sick and tired of being miserable? Don't you take enough crap from the world? Why do it to yourself? The voice in your head came from the voices of the abusers. Stop listening to it. Train yourself to be good to you and to speak kindly to yourself always.

23. https://en.wikipedia.org/wiki/Stuart_Smalley

Affirmations are empowering positive statements that you repeat to program your subconscious mind to produce different and positive behaviors. Eric Butterworth[24] states that we don't repeat affirmation to make them true. We repeat affirmations to ALIGN our consciousness with the truth.

Why is this so? Saying these positive statements with conviction helps to restructure our subconscious to believe what we are repeating. The subconscious mind cannot discern between an imagined experience and a real experience. It just takes in information you give it, decisions you make, and drives your behavior based on that input. If you want your behavior to change, you must align your subconscious with your new ideas, or it will keep churning out the same old behaviors you've always had.

Affirmations, specifically the constant repetition of the new operating instructions, are what give the subconscious its marching orders.

When you begin to do this, the subconscious will erect barriers to your progress. This is the brain trying to protect us. "Whoa, wait a minute. That's not what we're supposed to be doing." And your mind will rebel. It will try to convince you that you are in danger. It will make you afraid to move forward. Be patient with yourself, and as you continue to repeat the message, the mind will relent and begin operating under the new directions.

The phrase "I am" is one of the most powerful things a person can say. Be careful what you say after that phrase because it defines who and what you are. Wayne Dyer[25] and Joel Osteen[26] write about that. When you talk about yourself and give the subconscious mind the direction "I am," it produces the characteristics and behaviors required to fulfill that direction "I am."

24. Butterworth, Eric, *Spiritual Economics: The Principles and Process of True Prosperity*, 1983, Unity School of Christianity, Unity Village, MO, 217 pages.
25. https://www.drwaynedyer.com/
26. https://www.joelosteen.com/Pages/Home.aspx

As a recovering victim, you can begin to change your view of yourself by starting to tell the truth about yourself. Let's examine the phrase, "I am stupid." Are you stupid? Or did you just do a stupid thing? In this first sentence, you are labeling yourself as a sub-par human being. In the second one, you are saying you made a mistake. Everyone makes mistakes. That makes you equal to all other humans in the world.

Remember that what you focus on gets stronger. If you want to maximize your strengths, focus only on what they are. Don't pay much attention to your weaknesses. What people learn playing racquet sports is, "Yes, you just missed that shot. Now focus on the next one." You can't move forward if you are always focused on what you did wrong in the past. Let go of the mistake and look at what you can do that is right, right now.

If your mind argues with you when you repeat an affirmation, use the following technique: Say the phrase, "I look forward to…" in front of the affirmation. Your mind cannot argue with the fact that you are looking forward to the day when you love yourself.

Here are some examples of affirmations you might want to say to yourself:

- "I am a winner." Think of all the things you did right today instead of what you did wrong. If your mind balks at this, say, "I want to be a winner," or "I look forward to believing that I am a winner." Keep repeating that until your mind stops arguing with it, and you can just say, "I am a winner."

- "I am lovable." If you don't think you are lovable, begin doing lovable things. Every time you remember a lovable thing you did, write it down. Make a list that you can read that gives you empirical proof you are lovable.

- "I am beautiful." Get your hair and nails done. You don't have to look like a movie star. Just look as good as you can. Happiness and a genuine smile make everyone look great. Begin to do things that make you happy, and you will be beautiful.

- "I know how to get what I want in life." If you don't think you know this, say: "I look forward to knowing how to get what I want in life." Begin to learn how to get what you like. Take a class; ask for help. You've made a good beginning by reading this book.

- "I am the master of my fate." Again, if you can't believe this, use the technique above.

- "I attract fulfilling relationships." Make a firm decision not to let anyone into your life that doesn't respect you, even if you have to wait a long time and be alone. Eventually, you will develop friendships with people that show you respect and love.

- "I have a healthy and fit body." It may not come easily in the beginning. This could take a long time. Don't get discouraged. Just continue to work on your fitness, and make it a priority.

Say affirmations out aloud and as if you believe them. Do something physical while you are saying them. It helps to anchor them in your body. When you move while repeating affirmations, your body is completely engulfed in the learning. Say your affirmations with feeling, allowing the feeling of them to become a part of your body. Visualize yourself in the situations you want to see in your life. Experience your affirmations as if they are happening right now. Allow the feeling to fill your body. Allow joy to infuse your thoughts as you speak.

Here is a physical movement you can do while you are saying your affirmations. Lift your right knee, and lower your left elbow to that knee. Now lift your left knee, and lower your right elbow to it. Do this while you are repeating your affirmations. It will boost your energy, engage your body, and strength the thought in your subconscious. It forces the energy to cross through the corpus callosum, the part that holds the two sides of the brain together.

Try to experience your affirmations several times a day. Repeat them in the morning before you are fully awake, immediately upon arising, or just before going to sleep.

Choose affirmations with the most personal meaning for you that are going to make your life the way you want it. The only rule is that it must be what you really want.

I have found that by recording my affirmations in my voice and listening to me say them has proved helpful. Sometimes, I say them as I listen; other times, I just listen in a quiet atmosphere. I have them recorded on my phone, so the affirmations are always handy.

Binaural Frequencies

Lately, I have been using audio frequencies to further healing. They seem to help me make the changes that I want to see with much less effort. I use them in conjunction with my affirmations, and my affirmations seem to work faster. Let's look at how the binaural frequencies work.

Neuroplasticity is the brain's ability to alter its physical structure, to repair damaged regions, to grow new neurons, and remove old, unusable ones. The brain also has the power to rezone regions of the brain that previously performed one task and use those neurons to perform a new task. The brain can change the circuitry that gathers the neurons into the networks that govern member, sensory input, emotions, cognitive abilities like thinking and imagination.

It is only until recently that scientists believed that the brain didn't change once the child reached adulthood. Recent scientific advances tell us that this is simply not true. The brain can and does change throughout our lives. It is adaptable, and like plastic, it adapts as we learn and grow. Hence neuroscientists call this "neuroplasticity "

The brain creates billions of pathways for neurons to travel. Each time your brain performs a task like thinking, feeling or moving, the pathway lights up with electrical current as the synapses fire off. Your habits cause certain paths to be more active than others. Something you think about or feel or do on a daily basis establishes a well-worn pathway through the neural networks. These are your habits. These behaviors are well-established and strong. This is called your comfort zone.

To develop a new habit, you may use a different neural pathway. This is why when you are doing something new or learning something new your head may hurt. It's just like a muscle that hurts when you use it more than normal. You are carving out a new pathway, and it takes a lot of energy to force the neurons into a new pathway.

Giving up a habit may be difficult because your brain is accustomed to the old behavior. The neurons just naturally move along the path of least resistance. Forcing them into a new pattern feels awkward. As you continue to force the thoughts into the new path, the old one becomes less used and weakens. The new path takes over and the impulses move more easily through it.

This process of rewiring the brain by weakening old connections and strengthening news ones is neuroplasticity in action!

We all re able to learn or change, by rewiring our brains. If you have ever learned something new or released a habit you have created new pathways in your brain utilizing neuroplasticity. Repetition is key to neuroplasticity. They more you repeat the thought, feeling, behavior the stronger the neural pathway becomes.

You can see the neural impulses on an electroencephalograph (EEG). This device can sense the electrical activity on your head and a needle on the machine can delineate lines on the paper that look like waves. That's actually where the term "wave" in brain wave comes from.

These wave patterns are closely related to your thoughts and emotion.

There are mainly five categories of brain wave patterns. The most rapid is called a Gamma brain wave pattern. This frequency is when you are functioning in your Genius Mode. The lowest brain wave pattern is called Delta. This frequency is vital for the release of your human growth hormone. The delta pattern appears more when a person is in a very deep meditation.

The five levels of brainwaves are:

Gamma Waves (31-100 Hz) – Peak Performance

Beta Waves (16-30 Hz) – Alert/Working/Stress

Alpha Waves (8-15 Hz) – Relaxed Focus

Theta Waves (4-7 Hz) – Internal/Integrative Focus

Delta Waves (0.1-3 Hz) – Deep Meditation

Scientists have discovered that your internal brain waves are impacted by the energy outside the body. You can notice this when you are in a good mood and you get involved with a person or group of people who are in a bad mood. Your brain will begin to adjust to the external energy, and you may find yourself in a bad mood and you don't know why.

Using binaural frequencies, you can change the frequency of your brain to elicit peak performance. I have been using these frequencies for about a year. They have helped me in subtle ways to increase my performance at work, in my personal life, and in my business. I find that I am far more productive and spend time with people who are operating at a higher level than I am. I am so grateful that these folks allow me to play on their level.

When your frequency aligns with the frequency of a certain feeling you can't help but attract that feeling and people who live with that feeling. It's why people in groups make about the same amount of money, weigh about the same amount as each other. We just naturally aggregate because out frequency attracts us to one another.

Look around you. Do you like the people you are spending time with? Do they uplift you? Or do they bring you down? If you are not happy with the group you are in, understand that you are the one who is attracting them. Raise your frequency in any way you can in order to find supportive and caring friends.

I did this and most of the old group just faded away. Now I have wonderful friends who treat me the way I deserve to be treated.

Not everyone who creates these frequencies is doing it correctly. I highly recommend Dr. Jussi Eerikainen's work *Transforming Vibes, Transforming Lives!: How to Tune Your Inner Frequency From Comfort to Ultimate Success*. He created a program *Your Genius Code Unlocked*, which provides the frequencies that I use.[27]

---

27. I receive no compensation for mentioning this.

Healing the Post-Traumatic Stress

Most of us who have been abused struggle with post-traumatic stress. You may think that you don't have it. I had no idea that I had it. I just thought I was overly emotional. A good trauma therapist was able to get me to see what was going on with me.

I used to always take recommendations from friends for therapists like other women get recommendations for hair stylists. In my late fifties, I made an appointment with a therapist that friends recommended. It turned out that he treated trauma. Not knowing what that was, since my mind was addled by trauma itself, I listened to him without understanding a word he said. I stayed with it for over a year.

He didn't know anything about alcoholism or addiction as I'm learning most trauma specialists don't. Surprised that a therapist today wouldn't be involved with that, I addressed his curiosity about recovery from alcoholism.

The upside to his lack of knowledge about alcoholism was that he gave me new ideas. When most therapists find out that you are an alcoholic or addict, they immediately funnel you into the addiction model. I didn't need that. I was almost thirty years sober at that time. He broadened my vision about what happened to me, and what I could do about it.

I worked with him for over a year as he tried to get me to understand my problem. He explained post-traumatic stress (PTS), and I listened…in vain. I was not getting it. Finally, after a year of listening, I was having yet one more emotional meltdown right there in his office, when he said to me, "That's it! What you are doing right now is having a PTS flashback." I thought the behavior he pointed out was just part of who I am. I'd watched it happen to me all my life. It was just a meltdown. I'd get over it.

The long hours of explanation must have finally worked because I saw for the first time, and in real time, what he was talking about. I could finally see that the emotional outbursts and misery were triggered from something that forced me into a past life experience. I wasn't just remembering; I was thrown into a place in my mind where I was reliving the episodes in my life. I wasn't an adult remembering. I was a six-year-old again actually re-experiencing the trauma. I could be trapped in those episodes for weeks and months at a time. There was no telling how long it would last.

Once I saw it, I couldn't unsee it. In that moment, my recovery from post-traumatic stress began.

IDENTIFYING TRIGGERS

One of the most important things I did was to identify what my triggers are. Once you become aware of what your response is to trauma, you can begin to identify when you have been triggered.

My response to a trigger was generally massive upset and weeping or an overwhelming sense of shame or guilt. I would take on shame or guilt in response to someone else's behavior. I would respond to their behavior as if I had performed the shameful or bad action. Since my role was the scapegoat, my family trained me to take on the shame and guilt for them. This spilled over to everyone in the world. That is a heavy burden for a little girl.

I am attracted to bullies like a moth to a flame. At once, I loved them, found them irresistible, yet reacted to them with fear, anger, sorrow, and loneliness. Any authenticity disappeared in their presence. The longer I lived with them, the deeper my authenticity disappeared deep within me until I didn't know I had any at all. That's when the weeping would begin.

Over the years, after I became aware of what my reactions were, I was able to identify what types of behaviors would set me off. I was able to prepare myself when in the proximity of the types of people and situations that triggered me. Once I began to identify the triggers that set me off, I became adept at recognizing dangerous territory and side stepping them. I learned how to ground myself in the moment in the room I was inhabiting so I could bring myself back quicker and quicker.

I saw traditional talk therapy exacerbated the problem. By continually repeating the old story, I kept getting caught in the flashback, and I reacted to it every time. I just found myself stuck in the story, spinning my wheels.

Even now I sometimes get triggered, but I recognize it quicker; and if I need to, ask for help quicker.

And in the spirit of full disclosure, even if you are in touch with your triggers, something could come up right out of the blue that just flies up in your face, especially if the trauma occurred at a very young age before you had any words for it.

Other People's Energy can Trigger a PTS Episode

I am highly sensitive to another person's energy. I had an experience that clearly showed me I must protect myself from other people.

One day I was in line at the grocery store. There was a woman in front of me who was creating a chaotic scene with the clerk. She was hyper and talking fast. It went on for some time, and I could see how frazzled the clerk was getting. What I couldn't see was that this woman was also making me a wreck.

When she left, I was actually dizzy. I commiserated with the poor clerk and went on my way. By the time I got to my car, I was hyperventilating and feeling super weird. My skin was crawling, and I was ready to scream. I wanted to cry; I wanted to run away. I finally called a friend and she talked me down. I thought I was crazy.

What I realized was that I allowed myself to be invaded by someone else's energy without ever knowing it. I did this all my life. I lived with other people's crazy feelings, or sadness, or fear, thinking it was my own. Now that I have lived alone for a long time, I have a good sense of my own energy signature, and I am able to recognize when foreign energy is coming into me.

I have learned to have strong boundaries, both psychological and energetic, so that I am only living with what belongs to me.

As abuse victims, we were not allowed to set boundaries. Strong psychological boundaries create strong people. We are not meant to live someone else's life. We fail at doing that, and it is the RIGHT thing to fail at.

I lived with an undercurrent of fear. I didn't know it was there until it was gone. I now call it my continuo in a piece of baroque music. It played in the background of my mind, always there, always providing the base from which I made all decisions. It kept me on edge and hyper vigilant even after other aspects of the PTS were gone.

More Techniques to Dispel PTS

There are several techniques that dispel the fear.

Praying for People You Resent

This technique is a powerful tool. I learned it through the 12 steps. The Bible talks about "praying for those who despitefully use you." It works. I don't know why. I don't care why. I just know it does. And most of us don't do it, until our ASSES are on FIRE. This is what you do. For two weeks, pray for the person who is annoying you, asking God to give them all the spiritual blessings God has for you.

The first time I did this, I thought I was going to choke on my words. "I'm not praying for that son of a bitch!" But I had to do it because I was miserable. My first prayer was, "God bless that son of a bitch before I kill him." You start from where you are. What I found out was that it doesn't necessarily change them, however, it does release the resentment from me. Like I said, I don't know why or how. I just know it does. All you can do is try it. If it works, use it.

And it can also change the other person. When I got that shiny new job at 65K, it came with a manager with borderline personality disorder. OMG, I was in hell. Every day I had to get on my knees and pray for him. After six months of misery, one day it all broke. I was in a meeting with him and my colleagues, and he called me on the carpet in front of them. And he was wrong; I hadn't done what he was accusing me of. I was going on vacation the next day, so I had all week to brood on it. When I got back, he walked by my office, and I called to him. I told him that he didn't have to respect me or even like me, but he could never again speak to me that way, especially in front of my colleagues. He broke down and said that he knew that was wrong, and he felt bad about it all week. He apologized, and we were great coworkers after that.

Holy shit! You could have pushed me over with a feather. This stuff works.

RECALLING ENERGY FROM BULLIES

I learned this technique from several different sources. It's called a couple of different things – "removing foreign energy from yourself" or "recalling your energy from others" or "releasing energy cords." This is how it works.

Make a list of people who are irking you. One by one, do this technique.

Picture yourself standing facing each person. Using your higher faculty of imagination, see a cord of silver energy stretching from the middle of your forehead to the middle of theirs. Do this at the hollow spot between your collarbones, the middle of your chest, and the middle of your belly just above the umbilicus. Now order all the energy that belongs to them and only to them that you have in your energy field to go across the cord to them. Once you sense it is complete, that all their energy is gone from you, call all your energy and only your energy that they have in their energy field back to you through the cord. Once you sense it is all back inside your energy field, cut the cord, and let it drop. This works even if the person is dead.

Do this with as many people as you need to. Do it more than once with a person if you need to. This is a powerful tool. This is how you can use your imagination to benefit yourself, instead of using it to scare the shit out of yourself with negative imaginings that rarely, if ever, come true. Don't allow your imagination to drain you of vital energy.

If you feel awkward doing this, just remind yourself that it is only an old paradigm making you feel that way and trying to keep you in a lower frequency.

Analyzing Dreams and Visions

Analyzing dreams is a great way for traumatized people to discover their authentic selves. Dreams tell you much about the things in your life your conscious mind cannot engage. They reveal in symbols what is terrifying.

I had one particularly astute therapist when I was in graduate school, one of the only two therapists who really helped me. She was a Jungian analyst, and I learned much from her. Our dreams are windows into our subconscious, and dream analysis forms the basis of Jungian analysis. By helping me understand my dreams, and my visions, she helped me emerge from the depths of my chaotic, punitive, rageful thoughts and feelings.

My dreams, always weird, and weirder during times of stress, provided her with fodder for her analysis. I had a lot of dreams about people trying to put out a little flame that I was protecting. Somehow it was vitally important that I protect that tiny blue flame. I came to learn that it was my own small and dim life force. Protecting it as if my life depended on it was the right thing to do–because it did.

I also had a lot of dreams about talking to severed heads. These heads were sometimes of people I knew, sometimes not; they would talk to me, and I wasn't afraid of them. She helped me discover that I was cut off from my body. "You are totally up in your head. You need to connect to your body." I had always been a walker, but at that time, I began to make exercise a priority. I played squash four to five times a week at the local squash club. I was in great shape. But not connecting with your body is more than a lack of exercise. It is an inability to engage yourself as an entire being. Having spent so much time in academia and using my intellect, I still struggle with connecting with myself on a visceral level.

If you choose to go into traditional therapy, I recommend only going to a trauma specialist or a Jungian analyst.

> *"Limitless power is God's gift to you*
> *because it is what you are."*
> ~A Course in Miracles

PRACTICE GRATITUDE

Rather than focus more on what you don't have, focus on all that you do have. Develop an attitude of gratitude, as the saying goes. Get in the habit of writing daily in a gratitude journal. Simply writing down the things for which you're grateful can make a substantial difference in your overall attitude toward yourself and life.

Practice gratitude so that you can feel grateful. Eric Butterworth wrote that gratitude is not a feeling; it is an action that is causal. You must "do" gratitude before you can "feel" gratitude. Each day, make yourself grateful so you can have that feeling of gratitude.

There is a process called the Rampage of Appreciation. In the Rampage of Appreciation, you look at or think of something that you love. You focus on the feeling the object gives you until it fills you up. Allow yourself to amplify that feeling until you are so exhilarated by it that you can feel joy throughout your body.

STOP COMPARING YOUR INSIDES TO SOMEONE ELSE'S OUTSIDE!

When you compare yourself to others to determine if you are smarter, better looking, and so forth, you deny your own right to be who you really are. Besides, you aren't seeing what they are going through on the inside.

This was a big one for me. I compared myself to everyone and felt less than. And I thought the world was concerned about, and critical of, everything I said and did. Well, guess what? The world has better things to do than to pay attention to my hairstyle, weight, car style and so on. You can help get past this adolescent mindset by deliberately changing your thought patterns.

There's a saying, "You wouldn't worry about what others think of you if you knew how little they do." Cold but true. You might be a blip on their radar that quickly passes, and they are back to thinking about themselves.

People are so busy thinking about themselves that they really don't have much room to think about you. Don't worry about them. Think about what you can do each day to feel good about yourself. To have good self-esteem, do things that produce good esteem. Do things that make you feel good about yourself.

We all make excuses for doing that which is bad for us. Begin to let go of the excuses you use. Accept that you are doing the behaviors. I am doing X. The truth will begin to set you free. Do not give in to excuses. Don't beat yourself up. Just accept what you are doing. It will free you to make a clear-headed decision.

Avoid Negativity

Seeing things negatively is a learned behavior. You can train yourself to stop looking at things negatively and to focus on the positive. Things have a better than equal chance of turning out good as they do bad. Forget Murphy's Law. Expect positive things. Cut off as many avenues to negativity as you can.

- Avoid negative people and situations
- Limit time spent watching the news

- Visualize good things happening
- Find people you like who are good, kind, and respectful, and spend time with them
- Practice saying nice things to yourself
- Reward yourself when you do things to be proud of

SEEK OUT LIKE-MINDED PEOPLE

Surround yourself with positive, supportive people who believe in you, encourage you, and have similar beliefs and values. Being around people with positive energy will energize, motivate, and inspire you, increasing your self-confidence. Most people earn within twenty percent of what their peer group earns and weigh within twenty percent of their peer group's average. Surround yourself with people who have what you want. Tennis players won't often play with people who are substantially worse players than they are because it can derail their game.

Up your game. Find people who will challenge you to be better than what you are today.

GROW SPIRITUALLY

Learn to forgive. When we encounter someone who has wronged us, our bodies tense up, and our mind fills with rage. Anger, resentment, and desire for revenge engulfs us. It says in *Twelve Steps and Twelve Traditions*,[28] an AA study book, in the tenth step, "It is a spiritual axiom that every time we are disturbed, no matter what the cause, there is something wrong with us." If someone is "pushing your buttons," you need to disable the buttons inside you that they are pushing. Identify why you are disturbed. It's most likely that you are seeing behavior in someone else that you detest in yourself. I know. It just sucks to hear that. Let yourself off

---

28. *Twelve Steps and Twelve Traditions: A Co-Founder of Alcoholics Anonymous Tells How Members Recover and How the Society Functions*, AA Grapevine, Inc. and AA World Services, 1952, 1953, 1981, 192 pages.

the hook for your imperfections. Stop disliking yourself. Do whatever you need to do to forgive yourself.

I talked about the forgiveness technique above, "I forgive myself for judging myself as…" Use it often.

Try to understand that when someone is unkind and heartless, it's a result of their own unhappiness. Let go of anger and resentment and move on. Forgive others, and forgive yourself for your transgressions, practicing self-compassion.

Practice Compassion

Acts of kindness and compassion sent out will come back to you. What we give, we receive. Practice the Golden Rule always – do unto others as you would have them do to you. Don't do to someone else what you would not want done to you. Every day do at least one kind act: compliment, volunteer, do something to help someone else.

Realize that everyone is fighting a battle you know nothing about. When they lash out, it is from their pain. It has nothing to do with anyone outside themselves. That doesn't mean you have to move in and live with them.

Be Kind but Take No Shit – Practice Assertiveness

While we need to practice compassion and forgiveness, we must never allow people to bully us. We must stand up for ourselves.

My father and sister were bullies, and I cowered before them. After I left the house and started to realize I could make it on my own without them, I became more courageous.

One incident of note happened in my early twenties when I went back briefly to live with my family. My parents neglected my little sister's dental health. When we moved to Florida, both my parents were working hard; and they stopped taking us to the doctor or the dentist, not because they didn't have the money, but because they were focused on their new business and too lost in their own struggles to care. My little sister lost most of the teeth on one side of her mouth by the time she was twelve.

One night we were all in the family room, and the subject of the dentist came up. I said to my father that I thought he should pay to have my younger sister's teeth fixed. He stood up and got all huffy. When I repeated it, he puffed out his feathers and yelled, "Shut up before I knock you on your ass."

Having been out in the world and kicked around a bit, I was no longer the wimpy, milquetoast he knew. I stood up and looked him right in the eye and said, "Go ahead. Take your best shot!" I had never stood up to him before. He stopped dead in his tracks, shocked by my reply. He turned and left the room. Wow! What a great feeling I had. I had finally stood up to the old man AND WON!

The next victory came a few days later when my mother, my older sister, and I were together. I was telling my mother about a job that I'd applied for as a veterinarian's assistant. My sister fancied herself the "animal whisperer." She was appalled to learn that I was "stepping on her turf," so to speak. She stood up and said to me, "What are you doing that for? You are too stupid to do a job like that." I looked at her and said, "Fuck you! Leave me alone."

Her jaw dropped open. She fell back into a chair and sat in stunned silence for about ten minutes. Finally, she jumped up out of the chair, left the house, and didn't return during the rest of my visit. She was not to speak to me for the next twenty-five years. I didn't care; I had finally stood up for myself.

It is a wonderful thing to do. Yes, if you stand up to bullies, you will get a backlash. In my case, both bullies never spoke to me again. That was a blessing and a curse. It is hurtful to be abandoned. I had to learn to be there for myself no matter what. I also learned that most bullies are paper tigers. If you stand up to them, they generally leave you alone, especially if you do it in front of other people.

I'm talking run of the mill bullies, not sociopaths. With sociopaths, you must get away as fast and as far as possible. If you are in danger, ask for help from professionals.

THOUGHTS THAT DON'T SERVE US

Here are some thought patterns that you need to change if you want to grow out of being a victim.

MAKING SHIT UP AND BELIEVING IT!
STOP CATASTROPHIZING.

If there is a fancy word for this, I don't know what it is. I spent a lot of my life doing this. Something happens. I have little to no information about the situation, but I make up elaborate stories about it in my head, based on almost nothing, AND THEN I BELIEVE THEM! And these stories always describe the most negative and catastrophic events possible. And what's worse, I would act on those stories as if they were true because in my mind they were true. I spent many hours, days, weeks in turmoil because I simply made up a story and believed it.

The other day, I was carrying a drinking glass. I had my palm over the top of it. I leaned down on it slightly for a second. In a split second in my mind, I saw the glass shattering, the sharp edges of the glass lacerating my hand and cutting through the tendons. I went into surgery; I came home with a huge white bandage on my hand and invented a way for me to use the mouse on my computer, so I could still work. All in less than a second. That's how fast my mind can make up shit to which I respond.

Fortunately, I have learned to recognize when I've just made up a story that I am believing. I used to do that and be completely ignorant of what I did and would then spend a vast amount of time panicking, worrying, being depressed.

Recognize when you have done that, and just laugh it off. I was profoundly impressed with myself over the cut hand story. I congratulated myself on having such a quick and detailed imagination.

I will often say out loud, "I just made that up, and now I believe it!" This helps me to forget about it. I don't want to waste this imagination. I want it to be put to excellent use for my benefit.

> "*I've lived through some terrible things in my life,*
> *some of which actually happened.*"
> ~ Mark Twain

Use your imagination to help you, not drag you down. Your imagination is a powerful tool that you use relentlessly even in your sleep. Most of the time, we allow it to work against us. Use it to support you and uplift you. Your imagination can have you walking on the surface of the sun in a Nano second. It can plunge you to the bottom of the Marianas Trench. It can force you into hell.

Let your imagination take you to wonderful places and help you develop your limitless potential.

"Poor Me"

The first step in our journey in breaking free is to accept that as adults, we choose the relationship. Without this mindset, we stay stuck forever feeling a victim and blaming the abuser, which prevents us from breaking the pattern and moving on. The good news is that if you chose it, you can unchoose it. Accepting responsibility is your key to freedom.

This is not to say that we are at all to blame for what happened to us. However, it is our responsibility to grow past it, for taking the necessary steps to get well.

Of course, it's hard. After all, we never willingly asked to be abused, tormented, and harmed. Nor can anyone blame us for feeling a victim. We've been trained to respond as the abuser wants us to. Some, like me, were born into abusive or neglectful parenting. Others had it thrust on them later in life due to the mental illness or addiction of the abuser.

But no matter how you got there, wallowing in self-pity will get you nowhere. I know that all too well as I was stuck in "poor me" for years. You need to make another choice. You need to choose to walk away, never go back, and learn to be your own person. It's like having to choose between the blue pill and the red pill in *The Matrix*.[29] There will be days when you wish you had taken the blue pill to go back to sleep in the matrix. The red pill is the only way to healing. The red pill leads to truth, to reality, and a life of freedom.

When you feel a victim, you feel that outside forces control you. You feel that someone or something outside yourself is responsible for how you feel or what happens to you. When that mindset prevails, you do little to nothing to change your life because you feel it's out of your hands. You are stuck in victimhood.

To change, you must understand that you are in charge and in control of what happens to you. You can only feel this way if you eliminate excuses and denial and take responsibility for your thoughts and actions. Hell, yes, it's scary. Use that fear to create exhilaration and anticipation. Don't wallow in misery. That is a choice. "Pain is inevitable. Suffering is optional."

Do what you must to find a place for yourself. Let go of any "friend" that wants to hold you back. That person is NOT your friend. If any person has an agenda for YOUR life, get rid of him or her.

---

29. http://www.imdb.com/title/tt0133093/ The Matrix, 1999.

Do not blame others for poor choices that you make. Accepting the truth about yourself will set you free. Did I want to admit that my life was a complete failure? Hell, no. Yet accepting that I was a failure set me free from the prison of having to be right. There is a saying: some are born to be right, others to be happy. Being right feels good for about twenty seconds, and then the gates of hell clang shut, and you spend seemingly all eternity trying to defend your position. Let go of the need to be right; choose to be happy. Admit what is wrong with you. Those who care about you will applaud your bravery. Find people who applaud you. Get yourself a cheerleader, one who has your best interests at heart. I found my coach and never looked back. She believes in me when I can't. She is my anchor. She is my lifeline. She gently and firmly, yet relentlessly, urges me toward my highest good.

Commit now to the belief that you make things happen, not that life is happening to you. You are the master of your fate. *You are duty bound to take responsibility for your life!*

Welcome obstacles as an opportunity for personal growth. Try to see them as challenges. To quote Nietzsche, "That which does not kill us makes us stronger." Learn from your mistakes and move on. We always learn more from failure than we do from success.

Another Thought Pattern That Does Not Serve Us – "Bad Me"

When you demean yourself and call yourself names – "fat, stupid, lazy, etc." – you are focusing on what you dislike about yourself. What we focus on gets stronger. Yes, you might have some of those qualities; you also have good, strong qualities. Focus on those. Ignore the less desirable qualities about yourself, focus on the good qualities, and the good will grow, and the less desirable will fade away. When someone compliments you, do you diminish your positive qualities? I always told everyone how bad and horrible I was. If they said I was smart, I would say, "Yeah, but I'm terrible at math." I don't do that anymore. When someone compliments me, I say, "Thank you." Learn just to say, "Thank you."

If someone says you're smart, say, "Thank you. What a nice thing to say. You made my day." Allow yourself to feel good about you and even greater as you allow the other person to feel good about themselves! Enlightened people like to make others feel good. How do you feel when people don't appreciate the gift you've given them? Allowing someone to compliment you allows them to feel good about themselves. You are giving them a gift by appreciating their compliment.

When you wake up in the morning, before you are fully awake, repeat, "I love myself unconditionally." If your mind balks at that, say, "I choose to love myself unconditionally" until you can believe it. Your critical mind is not functioning in that half-awake state. You can feed your subconscious more easily from that place.

ANOTHER THOUGH PATTERN THAT DOESN'T SERVE – PERFECTIONISM

Perfectionism creates a false standard that is impossible to attain. When you fall short, as you must, you deride yourself for failing. As a result, you feel that you must do something perfectly or not at all. You're never good enough.

Such thinking makes it almost impossible to move forward and greatly impacts your life choices, making you feel anxious and depressed.

My parents never taught me anything but, at the same time, expected me to be perfect. Or if they were teaching me something, they expected me to be perfect at it from the first try. I learned to expect that of myself because if I did everything right the first time with no mistakes, maybe they would love me. Who can win with that as a goal? Of course, that never worked, and I always felt worthless, not good enough, someone who never should have been born. Eventually, I learned to accept my shortcomings and let go of the idea that I had to be perfect to be loved. As they say, "The best you are going to get to be in this life is human."

Expect Backslides

My journey was not smooth. Journeys never are. Often, I seemed to take one step forward and two steps backward. I would leave whatever abusive guy I was with only to go back to him or find another one as abusive and, at times, even more so.

This is normal. We all backslide. Finally, I said, "Enough! This has got to stop!" I used to call that step zero – the step you take before the first step you take toward yourself. I jokingly say that Step Zero is, "This shit has got to stop." That's not an actual step. I made it up, or more likely, I heard it somewhere and stole it.

Of course, even when you feel you have your life in control, things happen to make you feel you have regressed. This happened to me recently. I became involved in an organization for seven months run by a bully. Fortunately, I had enough recovery that I was able to function around her.

She became more aggressive and paranoid. Her pathological lying, which was always there at a low level, reached a crescendo that defied logic. Why lie, when the truth is simple? Pathological liars must lie; their brokenness makes them feel that their lives depend on keeping the truth hidden. I watched this behavior in my mother. I don't understand it, however, I respect it. Lying for them is a powerful protector, and you don't dare challenge it because they will sacrifice you before they will reveal their truth.

Seven months into working with this organization, I saw my typical responses starting to kick in. I began appeasing her, cajoling, walking on eggshells so as not to set her off. I watched as parts of me disappeared in her presence. She ruled with fear, and I was succumbing to it.

I realized I had to distance myself from her and left the organization. The oddest thing happened. When I woke up the morning after I quit, I COMPLETELY FORGOT what I was upset about. I tried and tried to remember why I decided to leave.

Fortunately, I had four other people who knew about the situation. I contacted them and told them my dilemma. They were able to remind me why I left.

How could I forget? What was going on in my mind that I just couldn't see the damage the broken person was causing me?[30] My brain shut off all logical thought.

This particular behavior occurred again and again in almost all my relationships. The storm would pass, I would recover, and I would forget why I was upset and from what I needed to protect myself. I would be in love again, or in friendship again, and it wasn't so bad, really. Until it happened again.

It has taken many years for me to become aware of this behavior. And thank God, I have. It was only because of having, for the very first time in my life, strong, connected relationships with powerful women who were going through the same thing and knew fully what was happening. I was able to trust them with my blank spot, and that trust enabled me to remember.

---

30. *The Body Keeps the Score: Brain, Mind, and Body in the Healing of Trauma*, Van der Kolk, Bessel A. – Penguin Books – 2015. P44 …our scans clearly showed that images of past trauma activate the right hemisphere of the brain and deactivate the left.

A NEW ME

My cruel family upbringing with alcoholic parents taught me the survival tactics of innovation and persistence. After leaving home at age eighteen and living on the streets as an alcoholic in New England, until I was "divinely guided" to go to college, I defied all odds and potential obstacles in my path to get sober. I earned a master's degree from an Ivy League college and a doctoral degree.

I owe my life to the higher power, whom I call God, who led me out of the chaos. However, I had to be willing to follow. Before I talk about God, and you turn me off, let me tell you everything I KNOW about God.

There is a God, and I'm not it!

That's the only thing I'm sure of. I'm not going to tell you what to believe. But I will tell you that you will need to find something bigger than yourself. My conception of God began with the thought that it was all powerful, all knowing, all loving, and it liked me.

I had never felt like people liked me. It was important that I had something in my life that liked me. Today I know that I live in a quantum soup of potential. The higher power, the Holy Spirit, Source Energy, Universal Intelligence, pure potentiality, Allah, God is there for all of us. It is like the sun that shines equally on everyone on the beach. I can have as much as I want because it is limitless. I can have as much freedom as I want without fearing that I am taking something from someone else. There is just as much for another as there is for me and you. Drink deep from the cup of grace. You can have all you are willing to accept.

All I can tell you is that I was sick and tired of being miserable. I became willing to do whatever it took to get well. I continue my quest for success and happiness. I don't know if I will ever find a life partner. I'm not worried about it. I am so happy being me.

My success at work has helped me greatly. In this post-human resources (HR), modern era, the rules in most work-places are beneficial to women: The rules are always the same. Clear boundaries exist around relationships between men and women, and I have been well rewarded for outstanding work. All this allowed me to become outspoken and clear in my communication at work, even when at home I remained the complete opposite.

The end of my "perfect marriage" brought more opportunity for my growth. With no experience whatsoever in the field, I embarked on a now more than twenty-year career in IT, and I developed my own successful consulting practice as an IT professional inside the beltway in the Washington, DC area.

The trauma and adversity I experienced caused me to search deep within myself for resources I would not have seen had I lived a stress-free life. I am grateful today that the fractures in my mind and my soul have been filled in with the "gold" of love and compassion. There is beauty where there was once agony. There is a sense of peace and joy, where there once was just confusion. As I let go of the judgment of myself, I judge others less and less. When I find myself judging others, I stop and ask what is going on in me?

I intend that my experience of a traumatic childhood and even adulthood can provide others with the hope that they, too, can overcome abuse and post-traumatic stress. With recovery as my life's calling, I hope my story can help people of trauma and abuse become willing to break free of past shackles and move forward in their lives. Nothing gives me greater satisfaction than to see others recover.

My greatest challenges inspired me to become the person I am today. My resilience enables me to make the best of every challenge.

I overcame a great fear of visibility to write this book because I am determined to reach out to others to encourage them to recover from their pain and suffering and become their best, truly authentic selves. And coming from the little girl who hid in the basement in the dark and ate, stepping out to tell my story to the world is a very bold step. It has taken me ten years to get the courage and recovery to do it.

For years I practiced in faith as I watched the techniques I described above help me unearth the real me. Through the psychiatric research that followed the end of the Vietnam war with soldiers returning mere shadows of the men they were previously, we now know a lot about the neuroscience of trauma. And doctors have been finding ways, non-traditional, non-pharmaceutical ways, of healing it. Pharmaceuticals have proven themselves ineffective in bringing people back from trauma. Medications will sedate a violent soldier, but they won't allow him to become who he needs to be.

This work saved me and gave me a life I couldn't conceive of as a child.

I have read many books, and I consider them the primary reason for my turning my life around. And though I could list and describe what I learned from each book, as they all had something unique to offer, in essence, they all say the same things. Our lives are all guided by the *Law of Vibration* and the *Law of Attraction*, some call it Karma, negativity attracts negativity; positivity attracts positivity. To change your thinking, you will have to give up false core beliefs that leave you stuck in a negative mindset and write a new script that you can impose on the neurons that are stuck firing in old, ineffective patterns. It may be difficult to imagine, but it will and must work for you as you raise your energy frequency to one of joy instead of misery.

A New You

Look for ways to free yourself from living in your inauthentic self. It requires dedication, focus, knowing what you want, and repetition to your subconscious mind informing it of the traits you want to develop. It is really frickin' hard; it is not as hard as living with the trauma. You are worth the effort you expend on your own behalf.

> *"Whatever you accept in your mind has reality for you.*
> *It is your acceptance of it that makes it real."*
> ~ A Course in Miracles

One of my deepest core beliefs was that I didn't have the right to make my own choices. In my life with my family, decisions were made for me. If I tried to think for myself, I was punished. I was taught to obey, no matter what. My job was to keep the peace. It didn't matter how negatively it impacted me; I was not to make waves.

Owning that belief was damaging to me. Once I owned the opposite, "I am 100% responsible for the course of my life," I began to have a sense of empowerment. If I caused it, I could change it.

What are your damaging beliefs? What do you tell yourself that works to sabotage you instead of helping you move forward? How would your life change if you were to take complete responsibility for all your actions and reactions?

The most important thing for our healing, without question, is the acceptance that we are 100% responsible for everything that happens to us. I hear you screaming at this one. No, you were not responsible for the trauma. You were not responsible for the fact that people treated you badly. That's on them, not you. Now it is your responsibility, no matter how unfair it may seem, for you to clean up the mess that they made of your life.

Nothing can change until you understand that your life is totally a creation of your own thoughts and energy. Yes, it is true that much of our lives as children were out of our control; once we become adults, it becomes OUR responsibility. We have the power to change even if all the brainwashing is telling us the opposite.

> "*As human beings, our greatness lies not so much in being able to remake the world,*
> *as in being able to remake ourselves.*"
> ~Mahatma Gandhi

> "*Everyone wants change; no one wants TO change.*"
> ~ Anonymous

Additional Information

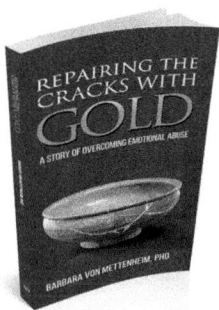

For more information please visit
Repairingthecrackswithgold.com

Facebook
**https://www.facebook.com/
Repairingthecrackswithgold/?ref=bookmarks**

Email
support@Repairingthecrackswithgold.com

About the Author

Dr. Barbara von Mettenheim holds a Ph.D. in English medieval literature. For over two decades, she has practiced personal development with the major thought leaders of the day. She discovered methods that freed her from her own personal past traumas and abuse.

Dr. Barbara was an indigent alcoholic. Her decision to get well allowed her to develop into an educated woman who raised a beautiful daughter and built a lucrative career. Now, she is a proud grandmother of two wonderful grandchildren (and hopefully still counting!)

She has identified effective methods that help liberate people from the effects of severe childhood abuse. In the process, she has helped people recover from post-traumatic stress, gain confidence, and develop resilient self-images to improve their performance in life.

As a lifelong learner, she continues to study and improve her life through the processes she describes in her book.

She lives just outside of Washington, DC.

Barbara has created a program designed to reduce the mental and physical symptoms of stress and trauma. Barbara will lead you through these processes and more to help you uncover the real you, relieve stress in real time, end faulty behaviors and thought patterns that continue to produce stress in your life, and help you move forward with confidence and joy.

Visit her website http://repairingthecrackswithgold.com.

With her brilliant business partner, Karrie Brazaski, Barbara helped create a program for nurses to relieve the stress of their jobs. Visit their website http://www.nursingnidra.com for more information on how they can support you in your journey.

www.ingramcontent.com/pod-product-compliance
Lightning Source LLC
LaVergne TN
LVHW051246080426
835513LV00016B/1758